Easter 1983

Dennis –
 I Believe in you –
 You are very special to me –
I know we'll enjoy reading
this together – we always do!

 Love you always –
 Annette

I Believe

I Believe

LOWELL L. BENNION

Deseret Book Company
Salt Lake City, Utah

To
   Ben
   Doug
   Steve
   Howard
   Ellen

©1983 Deseret Book Company
All rights reserved
Printed in the United States of America
Library of Congress Catalog Card No. 83-70024
ISBN 0-87747-954-2

First printing February 1983

Contents

Preface

The essays in this book present one person's view of certain aspects of the restored gospel of Jesus Christ. I have no intention of presenting herewith a systematic, comprehensive theology. My desire is to provoke thinking, to stir feeling, and to make the gospel more functional in our lives.

Abstract theology has its place, but it saves no one either in this life or in eternity. But our religious beliefs, when real and internalized, can sustain us through the vicissitudes of earth experience and enable us to face eternal life with confidence and trust.

It is my hope that these essays will help someone make religion more meaningful in everyday living.

Without holding anyone else responsible for the views expressed or errors made herein, I give much credit to friends, students, and kinfolk who have been free with their criticisms of both thought and form. I am particularly indebted to Emma Lou Thayne, Edith Shepherd, "Ben" Bennion, Ellen Bennion Stone, Lowell Durham, Jr., and the staff of Deseret Book.

Introduction

Why Examine Beliefs?

This book is a statement about some of my religious beliefs. My beliefs are important to me because they form the core of my personal philosophy of life. They determine in large measure my values, what is important in life, how I feel and how I act, how I cope with this mortal existence. My beliefs give direction, purpose, and meaning to my life.

But why should you, the reader, or anyone else—except my family and close friends—be interested in what I believe? It is my hope that my beliefs may give you some new insights into old ideas, but, more importantly, that my own statement of beliefs may cause you to reflect on your own, to assess what you believe, to clarify for yourself your own religious view of life. Your beliefs, though different from mine, serve the same purposes in your life as mine do in mine. They determine how *you* feel, think, and act.

Socrates said: "The unexamined life is not worth living." I might paraphrase his saying in this way: "The unexamined religious life is not worth having." Religion is not static in the life of the individual. It is not something like simple arithmetic, which we learn once and for all in childhood. To be vital, religion, like science, art, and philosophy, must be a growing, ever-learning experience.

The gospel of Jesus Christ is called unchanging eternal truth in contrast to the changing, tentative findings of science. Granted that the gospel of Jesus Christ is eternal truth because it is God's truth, this does not mean that I as a believer possess eternal truth. I do not understand—nor do you—the principles of God and Christ as they do. My knowledge of gospel teachings is limited by my ignorance, my sin, my mortal perspective. No matter how absolute truth may be in the mind of Deity, my understanding of God, Christ, humility, faith, and love is partial and relative to my experience and capacity. As Isaiah clearly states for God: "For my thoughts are not your thoughts, neither are your ways my ways, saith the Lord. For as the heavens are higher than the earth, so are my ways higher than your ways, and my thoughts than your thoughts." (Isaiah 55:8-9.) Recognizing our lack and need, the scriptural injunction to all of us is: "*Ask*, and it shall be given you; *seek*, and ye shall find; *knock*, and it shall be opened unto you." (Matthew 7:7. Italics added.)

What follows, then, is not my last will and testament. It is how I think and feel about some things in my religion today. My religion is not fossilized; rather, it is more like a living tree—not brittle like a chinese elm, its branches breaking in every wind and storm, but more like a sturdy oak with weeping willow branches grafted in.

There are fleeting moments when I wish I had the faith of a child. I hope my faith has retained some elements of a childlike faith—curiosity, openness, readiness to forgive, some trust. But I am not a child, and I can no longer think and feel as one. I have read books and have experienced tragedy, failure, sin, remorse, and doubt as well as thinking, learning, joy, and ecstasy.

Your life, like mine, is characterized by multiplicity and change. Religious beliefs provide an anchor that can give security, continuity, and direction to life. They provide aspiration, hope, purpose, and excitement to living.

But religion will do these things only if it is a dynamic, growing experience relating fruitfully to the whole of our feeling, thinking, and living.

The following essays, I hope, will stimulate thought, arouse feeling, and move us to action.

1

I Believe in God

In my judgment, one can neither prove nor disprove by rational arguments the existence or nonexistence of a God who has any meaning in the lives of human beings. There have been and are philosophers who believe in God, each according to his own perception; many others declare themselves to be atheistic or agnostic. In every field from science to art to the humanities, there have been and are those who believe and those who do not believe. Counter to every argument for believing, it seems, one can find an argument for not believing. So one's feeling for God becomes quite personal, based on one's total life's experience.

I believe in a personal God—an intelligent, sentient person who is concerned with human beings, who is seeking to achieve his purposes in their lives. While any description I may give of him is inadequate, because it is couched in human rather than in divine terms, still I believe man is enough like God—created in his image—that he can know in some measure the character and will of God.

Initially I was taught to believe, conditioned or indoc-
trinated by believing parents, neighbors, teachers, and
exemplars. This I admit is not a convincing argument for
the existence of God. People can be deceived. People are
taught untruths. I give it only as an honest reason for my
own faith.

This initial foundation of my faith has been tested
over and over again. At times I have doubted the existence of God. Sometimes I have felt that he has forsaken
me. At other times I have felt that he has sustained me
through the vicissitudes of life. But I have read books, listened to arguments, weighed both sides of the issue, and
through it all I have to this point come through with faith.
But I acknowledge that my faith is not absolute. No faith
is absolute. I do not know absolutely of God's existence; I
believe. I walk by faith. I trust him with a faith that I
would not trade for the professed knowledge of him.

My faith in God rests on two things: my total view of
the world and religious experience. When I contemplate
the order and beauty in the universe as I witness them in
the human body, in my garden, on my ranch in a valley of
the Tetons, or in the mountains of Switzerland, I find it
easier to believe that they are the work of a great creative
intelligence than to believe that they came about by
chance, by nonintelligent forces.

Creations reflect their creators. One of the surest bases
of my faith in God is my experience with the most complex of his creations, human beings. While some people
believe in man because they believe in God, my experience with people strengthens my faith in God. I have
known men and women and children whose brilliance of
mind, fine qualities of integrity and love, or masterful creations of art are such that it is easier for me to believe they
are from God, partakers of his nature, than it is to believe
that they have their ultimate origin in impersonal forces.
Man leads me to God even as the latter helps me to keep
faith in man.

W. P. Montague, an American philosopher, in his

book *Belief Unbound* has stimulated my thinking. He defines religion as "the faith that the things that matter most in life are not ultimately at the mercy of the things that matter least." He argues that if there is no God, then all the values that men cherish—truth, goodness, and beauty—are at the mercy of the cold, impersonal forces of nature. Without God, these values would perish with our own perishable selves. Even the tragic suggestion of such a thought does not, of course, guarantee God's existence. Human values such as freedom, integrity, love, and beauty are of great value, even if temporary, whether God exists or not. But I confess that my love for the values that I cherish and my respect for their great worth make me want to believe that they have cosmic support. That is the only sure way of guaranteeing their survival.

In addition to my view of the world that sustains my belief, I suppose the surest foundation for my faith in God lies in the area of religious experience. This is a very private, personal world that can mean little to anyone who has not had similar experience. Indeed, it is so private that it would be impossible as well as uncomfortable to try to reveal it on the printed page.

At various times, I believe I have experienced the power and influence of God in my life. I have been healed through private prayers; I have been confirmed in some very important decisions of my life; I have been comforted, strengthened, and reassured in critical situations by what I believe to be the witness of the Holy Spirit. I believe these experiences to be something apart from customary human experience. I realize how deceptive emotional states can be and how easy it is for one to impugn to Deity the psychological states that are determined by the interaction of an individual with his environment. I too may be fooled in my interpretation of what I believe to be divine manifestations to me.

However, I have known various emotional states. I know what it is to experience romantic ecstasy, aesthetic response, fear, anger, hope, compassion, praise, communion with the spirit of a friend. While they are perhaps not known singly or in their pure form, they do, each in turn, have a distinctive character. I agree with Rudolph Otto, who has said that religious experience—man's confrontation with Ultimate Reality—has its own unique character. I am not a mystic by nature, but I have had experiences that enable me to treat the experiences that mystics report of God with due respect and with the conclusion that they lie in the realm of possibility.

Jesus said: "If any man will do his [God's] will, he shall know of the doctrine, whether it be of God, or whether I speak of myself." (John 7:17.) I suppose the main reason I continue to believe in God is that I know for myself that the basic values and principles that Jesus and the prophets taught are true, that is, that they give meaning and fulfillment to life. I have witnessed their fruit in the lives of my fellowmen; I have experienced in a modest way the fruits of gospel living. I also know from my own experience and by observing others the consequences of violating the qualities of life Jesus taught. Jesus said, "Believe me for the very works' sake." (John 14:11.) This I do.

I have long felt that when one tries to live by the values in the Judeo-Christian tradition, he experiences divine support and affirmation. My faith is strongest when I believe I am doing God's will. As these values come alive in my associates, they bear witness to me of the divine influence operating in their personalities. Humility, penitence, moral courage, and love in human experience manifest to me the presence of God. "Where love is, there God is also," said Leo Tolstoy. And Romain Rolland in his great work *Jean Christophe* said: "If any man would see the living God face to face, he must seek him, not in the empty firmament of his own brain, but in the love of men."

Somehow I never doubt that God is on the side of freedom, justice, and mercy. My sense of his reality and of communion with him is strongest when I too—in my limited way—try to "do justly, and to love mercy, and to walk humbly with [my] God." (Micah 6:8.)

2

I Believe in Jesus Christ

Jesus of Nazareth is basic to my religious life. I am grateful to have been born after him and to know something of his life, teachings, and mission. In this chapter I shall discuss some aspects of his life that have come to mean much to me.

Master Teacher

He was a master in the art of teaching. An artist in story telling, he used parables so effectively that they alone stamp him as a great teacher. Creator of proverbs, he wasted not a word. Brilliant in dialogue, he was equal to every situation. Like many of the Hebrew prophets before him, his prose, as recorded by Gospel writers, was as beautiful and pregnant with meaning as poetry. His language was such that a child could understand some of his thought, yet so profound that scholars could ponder its meaning through the ages. Like Shakespeare, he spoke of things one can touch and see—lilies of the field, birds and foxes, lanterns without oil, the sun, salt, a yoke, a beam in one's eye, fish, the soil. His sayings are marked by both simplicity and profundity.

Jesus was positive in his teaching. His Beatitudes all begin with "Blessed are . . ." His great summary of religion, repeating the Old Testament, is altogether positive in its content and setting. "Thou *shalt* love the Lord thy God with all thy heart, and . . . thy neighbour as thyself." (Matthew 23:37, 39. Italics added.) His parables for the most part convey that same command to action. Think of the parables of the sower, the mustard seed, the good Samaritan, the prodigal son, the talents. Religion for Jesus was action born of faith and love. His positive emphasis is consistent with human nature, with man's need for creative self-expression.

Jesus taught by principle. He stressed and exemplified fundamentals of life and religion, leaving it to each generation to make application of his principles. Hence his teachings are timeless and universal in character. Had he taught a myriad of rules, his teachings would be as obsolete as is that of much of the pharisaism of his day. It is said that the only rule he ever laid down was his statement against divorce. Even in this instance, it may not have been his full view, but rather an appropriate response to a particular question put to him. (See Matthew 5:31-32.)

There is coherence, an inner-relatedness, in his sayings. His ideas presuppose, support, and enrich each other. They seem to evolve chiefly around integrity, love, humility, and faith. The first four Beatitudes, for example, are essential ingredients of integrity: humility, penitence, meekness, and hunger and thirst after righteousness. We cannot be *one* or *whole* without these virtues and other closely related ones that Jesus taught: sincerity, absence of pretense and guile, moral courage. Jesus placed these more personal virtues first in his "map of life" because they are prerequisite to the preeminent virtue of love. We cannot love our neighbor without first possessing integrity. Christ knew, as many students of human behavior have come to understand, that it is quite impossible for us to love our neighbor unless we have learned to love ourselves. And we cannot love ourselves if we are weak and divided. Unless one's own cup of life is full to overflowing, one has little to give to others. In fact, if one's own cup is half empty, chances are that he will try to use (or abuse) others in a futile attempt to fill his own.

Jesus taught that love is the matrix of life on which all other principles depend. He knew centuries before the behavioral scientists did that human beings need to give and receive love more than anything else after they have food, air, and water. We "live and move and have our being" in each other as well as in God. The last four Beatitudes— mercy, purity of heart, peaceableness, sacrifice—along with other "social" virtues, such as patience, kindness, courtesy, tolerance, long-suffering, and forgiveness, are but expressions of love.

Revelator of God

Jesus had implicit faith in God and his purposes, and he tried to inspire that same sense of trust toward God in men: "Wherefore, if God so clothe the grass of the field, which to day is and to morrow is cast into the oven, shall he not much more clothe you, O ye of little faith?" (Matthew 6:30.) On another occasion he said: "Believe me that I am in the Father and the Father in me: or else believe me for the very works' sake." (John 14:11.) My faith in God is strongest when I am engaged in the work of his Son, when I am trying to serve his purpose in a manner consistent with his character.

For me, Jesus is the revelation of God, the exemplification of the divine character. I can believe in the kind of God made known in the life of his Son. I reject characterizations of the Father, no matter where they occur, if they contradict the character and attributes manifested in Jesus Christ. Jesus has convinced me that God is an intelligent, just, merciful, forgiving, loving Father committed to the blessing of mankind.

Exemplar—Emissary

Max Weber, a great German sociologist and student of religion, classified the religious leaders of mankind into two categories. He called those of Asia, such as Buddha and Confucius, *exemplars*. Men followed them because they believed these teachers had found the way and exemplified that way in their own lives. These men were intellectuals who thought through life's questions and found answers.

Weber called the second category of prophets *emissaries*. Unlike the exemplars, these men believed themselves to be sent of God. They spoke for him. They were "God-intoxicated"—emotional, dynamic, human, often angry with their people. They were followed if and when men believed them to be spokesmen for God. Otherwise they were rejected and even stoned or imprisoned. The Hebrew prophets, Peter and Paul, Muhammad, and Joseph Smith were all emissaries.

The remarkable thing about Jesus of Nazareth is that he alone personified both types of prophets: exemplar and emissary. He is revered as the revelation of God incarnate. Particularly in the Gospel of John is he portrayed as the divine and perfect exemplar. "I am the way, the truth, and the life." (John 14:6.) "He that hath seen me hath seen the Father." (John 14:9.) In Matthew he tells us, "Come unto me, all ye that labour and are heavy laden, . . . take my yoke upon you." (Matthew 11:28-29.) One can follow Jesus for what he was, for the perfection and beauty of his life.

On the other hand, Jesus was also the great emissary. He dared to speak for God. He said, "Why callest thou me good? there is none good but one, that is, God." (Mark 10:18.) He came to do the will of him who sent him. He deferred to his Father with restraint and humility. I can follow him for what he is in his own right. I can follow him because he is the finest interpreter and emissary of the Divine Will and Purpose.

My Redeemer

In Christ Jesus lies my greatest hope and trust in personal immortality. In one sense, death is so convincing, so final, so beyond redemption that the resurrection wrought by the Christ, if real, ranks as the greatest of all miracles. "Why seek ye the living among the dead?" (Luke 24:5), words spoken to Mary on the morning of the third day following his burial, is among the most startling and dramatic declarations ever uttered. I am glad that I can believe, that I have hope in the resurrection. I am pleased to walk by faith in this glorious possibility of personal immortality.

I am living by the faith that one day I shall be privileged to meet Christ, to look into his face, to feel the touch of his hands, to hear words from his lips. I am comforted by the words of Jacob to the effect that "the keeper of the gate is the Holy One of Israel; and he employeth no servant there." (2 Nephi 9:41.) I would rather be judged of him than of men. I trust his justice and his mercy.

Christ came to redeem men from sin. Some people take a rather legalistic view of this dimension of his mission, thinking of him as a ransom for the sins of men who repent. I believe that Christ suffered for our sins, and that in some way unknown to me, his death can bring redemption from sin. But there are other aspects of his atonement from sin that for me are more understandable and of immediate application.

I am impressed by the words of Amulek concerning Christ's atonement: "This being the intent of this last sacrifice, to bring about the bowels of mercy, which overpowereth justice, and bringeth about *means unto men that they might have faith unto repentance.*" (Alma 34:15. Italics added.) Jesus lived, taught, and died that men might see the right, recognize their sins in its light, and be moved with faith unto repentance. Anyone who loves Christ and will serve him will find the power to repent. His sacrificial love inspires one to rise above sin. Christ suffered not only for our sins but because of them, as King Benjamin said: "For behold, blood cometh from every pore, so great shall be his anguish for the wickedness and the abominations of his people." (Mosiah 3:7.) Christ loves us so much that he suffers when he sees us ruining ourselves in shallow and destructive ways, knowing what our lives could be.

I have seen men transformed in this life by conversion to Christ and his way of life. I have learned through my own experience that I am stronger and less sinful when I am in his service than at any other time. He is indeed my Redeemer from ignorance, from death and from sin.

> *He marked the path and led the way*
> *And every point defines,*
> *To light and life and endless day*
> *Where God's full presence shines.*
> —Hymns, no. 358

3

I Believe in the Reality of Evil

One reason people have difficulty believing in a personal God is because of the presence of so much inequality, evil, and suffering in human life—and all of this in a world purportedly planned and created by a God who is all-knowing, all-powerful, and wholly good. How can a God who is good create a world with such an abundance of suffering?

Before responding to this question, let us consider first what inequality is. It is that persons are not equal in their capacity and/or in their opportunities to fulfill their potential. There are vast genetic differences among men and women. More than that, there are gross deficiencies that rob many individuals of the opportunity to live productive lives. I am thinking of grossly retarded persons and of children born so malformed as to exist only as "vegetables." There are also vast inequalities in the human environment. Some human beings are being born to remain ignorant, to be malnourished, or to be rejected and abused by unloving parents, through which experiences they suffer irreparable damage. Others are born of parents who nourish body, mind, and feeling.

There are two kinds of evil in which mortal existence abounds; both cause immeasurable suffering. The first type is called *natural evil*, which comes from destructive forces such as earthquakes, volcanoes, hurricanes, tornadoes, floods, and disease. These strike alike whoever chances to be in their path—innocent children, saintly mothers, or profaners of Deity. Natural evil is also evident in a great deal of animal suffering.

A second type of evil is called *man's inhumanity to man*. Hitler killed six million Jews in Europe. From the beginning, when Cain killed Abel, man has been at war with his neighbor. The question is, why did an all-wise, good Father create men and women with this capacity to be selfish and cruel? Why does God permit so much innocent suffering, suffering born of men's capacity to destroy one another? How can an absolute God who is good create human beings given to so much evil? There is also great physical and psychological suffering among human beings.

I am not unaware of values in human suffering. My pain makes me grateful when I become free of pain. It may also save my life and make me compassionate toward fellow sufferers. But I often see suffering—even from my limited perspective—go beyond any possible compensatory or redemptive value. Animals live in agony; little children suffer terrible pain; mature people through the ages have lain in excruciating torment, particularly before the availability of man-made pain-killing drugs.

I appreciate the order and beauty in nature and have always thought there was more good than evil in human nature, and I can allow for wisdom in permitting considerable suffering in human existence. But there is more inequality, evil, and suffering in the universe than I can ascribe to God, to the kind of God revealed in Jesus Christ. Nor am I satisfied with the traditional explanations that attempt to reconcile inequality, evil, and suffering with the all-knowing, all-loving, all-powerful God.

I know that I see life from the limited perspective of mortal man, that I do not see as God sees. I know that earth life is but a second in eternity. I know that man must walk by faith, as the author of Job concludes. But the same scriptures that tell us to trust God also hold us responsible for our deeds, and they place tremendous value on this moment of earth existence. They declare man's eternal salvation to depend largely on the quality of life here. They hold us responsible for our eternal destiny just as if everyone had an equal chance. (I am aware that those who grow up without the law will not be punished by the law, but neither are they blessed by it.)

Those who believe in an absolute God have various explanations for evil, inequality, and suffering. One answer is to deny their existence, to say that these things only appear to be present, or that, in reality, they are good in disguise. This point of view is preposterous to me. Inequality, evil—both natural and moral—and human and animal suffering are real, and they can destroy human beings both physically and spiritually. And they are frequently in greater abundance than is good for human beings.

Some apologists argue that God made men good but that he gave them free agency so they could become responsible for the evil they do. Even though this sounds like a good explanation of moral evil, it leaves me dissatisfied, because I cannot understand how man can be truly free and responsible if both his freedom and the environment in which he is to exercise it are wholly the creations of God. It seems to me that under these conditions, God would be ultimately responsible for what man is.

I hasten to acknowledge again that my ways are not God's ways, that my thoughts are not his, and that my logic and perspective may be utterly erroneous. Nevertheless, how can I make judgments except out of my capacity to think, out of my own experience, from whatever inspiration is available to me?

I am grateful for my concept of God learned from the restored gospel. It enables me to accept the reality of inequality, evil, and human suffering and yet provides me with a logic for believing that these things need not be ascribed to God. I can believe that the God whom I worship is just, good, and merciful.

In the Mormon view, God is not wholly responsible for nature or human nature, including man's agency. For God did not create all things: "Man was also in the beginning with God. Intelligence, or the light of truth, was not created or made, neither indeed can be. All truth is independent in that sphere in which God has placed it, to act for itself, as all intelligence also; otherwise there is no existence." (D&C 93:29-30.) Man's intelligence is coexistent with God. Man's free agency is an essential aspect of his intelligence—God-respected rather than God-created. Man is not entirely the creation of God, and his agency is inherent in his eternal intelligent nature. Deity has added to man's original nature through acts of creation, but God did not begin with nothing. Man, too, in some sense is an eternal being, without beginning or end.

Not only man's intelligence, but also aspects of nature are coexistent and coeternal with God. "The elements are eternal. . . . The elements are the tabernacle of God." (D&C 93:33, 35.) God is tremendously powerful in relation to nature. Like any builder, he must work with the materials and conditions that prevail. He is bound by the nature of the elements and of human nature.

Inequality and evil are not God-created; they lie in the nature of the universe and of man. God is wholly good, seeking man's best interest. Mormon bears witness to the goodness of God: "Wherefore, all things which are good cometh of God. . . . But behold, that which is of God inviteth and enticeth to do good continually; wherefore, every thing which inviteth to do good, and to love God, and to serve him, is inspired of God. Wherefore, take heed, my beloved brethren, that ye do not judge that which is evil to be of God." (Moroni 7:12-14.)

If the elements and their laws and man's intelligence, including his agency, are coeternal with God, then inequality and natural and moral evil are inherent in the very nature of things and are not the products of the Lord's creative work. Suffering is the by-product of the nature of things and of man's freedom of choice.

The Creator is doing all that he deems wise and efficacious to overcome evil, to help persons achieve their full potential, to diminish suffering. In the Mormon view, he needs and seeks our cooperation in his quest of the good life on our behalf. The human drama is still in the making. Its successful outcome depends on us as well as on Deity. He needs and calls for our cooperation. We must serve one another, be instruments of God for good.

I confess I do not comprehend God's ways with men and nature beyond broad principles. While man is an eternal, intelligent, potentially free entity, coeternal with God, I believe that he has always "lived, and moved, and had his being" in God. (See Acts 17:28.) We have had a measure of independence, but our eternal existence has also in some real sense been dependent on God, the eternal Father. This may also be true of nature, which, though eternal, and also in a measure independent, is in some sense dependent on the intelligent power and influence of Deity.

I glory both in man's independence and in his relationship to and dependence on God. I like the thought that life is real, that God cannot fulfill my nature without my cooperation, that he needs my help to achieve his loving purpose in my own life and in that of others. And I also glory in the faith that I am a child of God, have partaken of his nature, am of the same intelligent species, and that my destiny lies in him—my ideal, my guide, my Father. This dual nature of my life—that of cherishing independence and responsibility and yet standing in awe of my Creator—I owe to my Mormon upbringing, and I cherish it.

4

I Believe in Grace

Speaking long ago in a meeting in Switzerland, I proclaimed that a person must have faith, must repent, and must be baptized to enter the kingdom of God. My emphasis, in good Latter-day Saint tradition, stressed what an individual must *do* to gain eternal life.

A minister in the audience interrupted me in a heckling way by quoting Ephesians: "For by grace are ye saved through faith; and that not of yourselves: it is the gift of God: not of works, lest any man should boast." (Ephesians 2:8-9.)

Instead of acknowledging the large role of grace in the gospel of Jesus Christ, I became defensive and quoted James: "Even so faith, if it hath not works, is dead." (James 2:17.) "For as the body without the spirit is dead, so faith without works is dead also." (James 2:26.)

Catholics and Protestants rely heavily on the grace of Deity. For this very reason, perhaps, Latter-day Saints seldom speak of it but instead, as I did in Switzerland, speak more often of their own works.

The restored gospel of Jesus Christ is rich in the grace

of the Father, Son, and Holy Ghost. Recognizing the im-
portance that grace plays in our lives need not diminish
the significant role individuals play in their own salvation
through faith and works, but it should greatly enhance the
gratitude, the humility, awe, and love we feel toward the
gracious members of the Godhead.

What is the meaning of grace? In the Old Testament,
grace is used synonymously with favor. Noah and Abraham found grace (i.e., favor) in the eyes of God, as did
Ruth in the eyes of Boaz. It is in the New Testament,
under the influence of Paul, that grace takes on a more
profound and theological meaning as the power unto salvation from death and sin. Grace becomes a supernatural
gift, a free gift of the Father and Son, by which man is
saved and sanctified. The key idea is that grace is an unmerited gift, unearned, freely given from a gracious heart
to another person. We do not earn a gift. If we did, it
would be remuneration.

What do the Father and the Son give to us so freely?
King Benjamin had part of the answer when he said: "In
the first place, he hath created you, and granted unto you
your lives, for which you are indebted to him." (Mosiah
2:23. Read verses 18-24.) Life itself—this wonderful
human existence with its marvelous capacity to see, hear,
feel, laugh, weep, remember, imagine, think, love, as-
pire, dream, hope—is a gift. We do not have the power to
create ourselves. We owe our very being to Deity and to
earthly parents.

Before our mortal experience, God took our eternal,
uncreated, self-existent intelligences and gave them
spiritual birth. We became his sons and daughters. We
partook of his divine nature, which deepened our longings
to love, to create, to know, to be free. We became Godlike in embryo with a boundless capacity for eternal progression toward the realization of our divine natures. This
spirit creation, then, was an act and gift of God, born of
his love and of his desire to share his full life with us.

A third act of creation is likewise a pure gift of our Redeemer. Christ died that we might live—live eternally

with spiritualized, resurrected bodies. What price he paid, what suffering he knew, what love he expressed in bringing to pass our resurrection, no one can know or imagine. We believe, hope, trust, and are grateful to the Savior for our faith in the reality of life eternal, where body and spirit inseparably connected may come to a fullness of joy.

In addition to these remarkable acts of creation on our behalf, three special gifts are available to us in the gospel. The first is the light of Christ, which enlightens everyone born into the world, an influence that emanates from the Son and persuades us to seek the truth and the right. (See Moroni 7:15-16.)

The second is the gift of the Holy Ghost, which doubtless is universal in influence and available as a constant companion to those who are meek and lowly of heart and who have committed themselves through faith, repentance, and baptism to be disciples of Jesus Christ. Why should the Holy Ghost devote his existence to the service of human beings? His too must be the spirit of love. True, one must prepare himself to receive this great gift, but it still comes to us as grace—freely given for our blessing.

A third gift of the gospel is the holy priesthood. When I was a boy of twelve standing before the congregation and hearing my beloved bishop say that I was worthy to become a deacon, I thought I had earned the priesthood. Now I know that it is the power of God, his to withhold or to bestow. The sharing of his power and authority is also his to give. The most I can do is to make myself worthy to receive of his grace and to exercise his authority with love unfeigned. (See D&C 121.)

All men are sinners. All of us knowingly fail, either by commission or omission, to measure up to what we know to be right and to be God's will. Prophets of old, however, have given us assurance that though our "sins be as scarlet, they shall be white as snow" (Isaiah 1:18), and "all his transgressions that he hath committed, they shall not be mentioned unto him" (Ezekiel 18:22).

These promises are predicated upon repentance, for forgiveness of sin is available to a person only on that condition. This fact may lead us to believe that we can earn forgiveness. But this is fallacious reasoning. If we could earn forgiveness, if we could make our sins wholly right, there would be no need for mercy or forgiveness. Justice would reign; the law of compensation would prevail. Forgiveness has meaning only when there is a need to give, to bestow grace, to show mercy. This need seems ever present simply because we so offend Deity and our fellows. The core of the word *forgiveness* is *give*.

No one has portrayed God's graciousness toward the sinner as fully as did Jesus. Think only of three parables: the lost sheep, the lost coin, and the lost son. Think of the adulterous woman dragged before him for judgment. Think of all the sinners, publicans, and people despised among men who "drew near unto him for to hear him." Isaiah, Hosea, and Jeremiah had proclaimed God's mercy, but Christ revealed it in his life and death—"Father, forgive them; for they know not what they do." (Luke 23:34.)

Yes, we must repent to receive forgiveness and to forgive ourselves. But a merciful Father, revealed in and through a loving Son, is quick to forgive anyone who is ready and able to receive forgiveness. There is no more beautiful principle of the gospel than forgiveness, and no greater evidence of the statement: "God is love."

The gospel of Jesus Christ—its teachings as well as its gifts—has come to us freely from Deity through inspired men and Jesus himself. No one of us discovered faith, repentance, the Beatitudes, love, the character of God. These principles and concepts were revealed to us through human and divine sources that preceded us. I am constantly grateful to be living after Moses, Amos, Isaiah, Jeremiah, Paul, Alma, Joseph Smith, and, above all, Jesus of Nazareth. Life would have much less meaning without the messages of these prophets and without the story of Jesus' life and teachings while he lived in the flesh.

Revelation itself is also an act of grace, as is answer to

prayer. Why should God or Christ give heed to man's cry, except out of their gracious concern, their profound love and regard for us?

The greatest gift in the gospel is that of Christ himself, that he would come to earth and would live, suffer, die, and rejoice for and with us. "For God so loved the world, that he gave his only begotten Son, that whosoever believeth in him should not perish, but have everlasting life." (John 3:16.) How instructive and inspiring it is to follow the life of Jesus as it is related in the Gospels and in Third Nephi—to marvel at the insight and acumen of his mind, the depth of his compassion, the strength of his moral courage, his unfailing trust in his Father, and his humility before the Father. He was and is truly the Master Teacher, the Great Exemplar, our Savior and Redeemer, our brother and friend. His own life and teaching are the essence of grace. "It is more blessed to give than receive." (Acts 20:35.) "For whosoever will save his life shall lose it; and whosoever shall lose [give] his life for my sake shall find it." (Matthew 16:25.)

The notion that we earn everything we get in life is not true. Many things come to us from God and fellowmen unearned. The car I drive, the clothes I wear, the books I read, the orange juice I drink are gifts of the minds and hands of men and women who have gone before me. My very life and my days on the earth I probably owe to medical science as well as to God and my parents.

I have a large, productive garden that flourishes because my neighbors and I fertilize, weed, and water the crops. But in our pride, we forget that we did not create the soil, the sunshine, the water, the seeds. These things came to us, in the words of Parley A. Christensen, as "unearned goodness."

The political freedoms I enjoy in this country were not of my making. They have their roots in the prophets of Israel, the statesmen of ancient Athens, creative political philosophers, and the founders of modern constitutions in many lands. Political freedom has come as a precious, costly gift to me. My work and yours is to preserve it—to insist upon being governed by law, not by men.

A piano student will get nowhere without ardent practice, nor will he learn to play without a piano, compositions, and a teacher. Grace and works blend together, but many gifts, not only precede, but succeed and make possible individual merit and achievement.

In the restored gospel there is a beautiful blending of grace and our own efforts in the religious life. God gave us the gift of life, but its value to us will depend upon our love and respect for that gift—whether we shall waste it in shallow or riotous living or realize and fulfill our rich human and divine potential. Christ holds out forgiveness to us, but we cannot be whole, we cannot receive it, except by exercising faith and acting on the opportunity to repent.

There are occasions, many of them, that demand that we work as though everything depended on our own efforts. There are other times when it is well to remember the grace of God and Christ and that of so many fellow human beings who have gone before us and of others still living. Grace is indeed a large part of both the gospel of Jesus Christ and our human life. Without grace there would be no life and no opportunity for faith and works.

Giving is a law of life. The peach tree bears fruit for the good and the evil, and when it ceases to give fruit, it dies. A seed of wheat bears one hundredfold. We too were born to give. Only as we learn to be gracious—giving, forgiving, loving, merciful—can we achieve harmony with life and with God and his noble Son.

5

I Believe in Repentance and Forgiveness

A friend once told me that his wife had committed a grave sin many years ago and had been brooding over it ever since. Life held so little joy for her that she even threatened suicide. Her potential as a human being had seemingly come to rest. Because of her unhappiness and immobilization, she not only made life almost unbearable for herself, but for her husband and her children as well. Was there anything she could do?

Historians have pointed out the folly of fighting wars on two fronts as the Germans did in both world wars. The same logic applies to personal living. He who fights himself least has the most strength for the outside battle. Life is more of a battle than a ballet. There are external obstacles enough to overcome without being paralyzed by stumbling blocks within.

Shakespeare's Macbeth asked the question: "Canst thou not minister to a mind diseased, pluck from memory a rooted sorrow, raze out the written troubles of the brain, and with some sweet oblivious antidote cleanse the stuff'd bosom of that perilous stuff which weighs upon the human heart?" (*Macbeth*, V, iii, 38-43.)

I believe there is an antidote to sin and failure. Some of it lies in common sense, and the rest can be found in the gospel of Jesus Christ.

As Aldous Huxley put it: "Chronic remorse, as all moralists are agreed, is a most undesirable sentiment. If you have behaved badly, repent, make what amends you can and address yourself to the task of behaving better next time. On no account brood over your wrong doing. Rolling in the muck is not the best way of getting clean."

We have learned that there is no strength in weakness, no power to repent in sin. We do not overcome our mistakes by being preoccupied with them. We succumb to that which occupies our minds and feelings. I agree with Huxley that it is pointless to rehearse past failures and sins.

This commonsense approach does not suffice for my friend's wife. Her belief in the gospel of Christ has only increased her burden of guilt. And even though she has repented of her sin, it bears her down in much the same way as I have seen an overload of sheaves weigh down a rickety old cart in Jerusalem.

This woman believes the gospel, but she does not understand the principles of repentance and forgiveness or the feelings of the Father and Son toward the sinner. None of us fully comprehend these things, but enough can be understood to bring comfort and hope to a person suffering from destructive guilt.

It is important to comprehend the fact that God does not love as most of us do. We are prone to love people whom we like and respect and who love us. Our love is conditional; God's is not. I remember a woman in her thirties who was finding it very difficult to accept herself and to feel comfortable in social relations. She recalled that when she was a little girl, her mother kissed her good night only if she had done nothing wrong during the day. The mother's "love" was dependent upon circumstance.

God's love, by contrast, does not have to be earned or merited. He loves us because it is his nature to love. No matter what we do, he still loves us, and he always distinguishes between the sin and the sinner.

When we sin, the Father and the Son feel pain because they love us. They know that sinning is destructive to our lives and to the lives of others. Likewise, when we repent, there is rejoicing in heaven because our lives have become whole again. This is beautifully portrayed in three parables spoken by the Savior: the lost sheep, the lost coin, and the lost (prodigal) son.

The setting that gave occasion to these parables is interesting. Even though Jesus was pure in his own life, publicans and sinners "drew near unto him . . . for to hear him." (Luke 15:1.)

In his parable of the lost sheep, Jesus made a surprising statement: "I say unto you, that likewise joy shall be in heaven over one sinner that repenteth, more than over ninety and nine just persons, which need no repentance." (Luke 15:7.) This idea puzzled me for a long time, because it appeared to show partiality to the sinner. Then one day my son grew so ill that I came to understand the meaning of this parable. I learned that *in the day my son's recovery was assured,* there was more rejoicing in our household over him than over our other children who were well. This did not mean we loved him more, but only that in the relief of his being "returned," we felt exquisite joy. The same joy would be experienced over a person who would "come unto himself" and return to better ways of living.

When the prodigal son, who had "wasted his substance with riotous living," came to himself and returned home, his father, who saw him "yet a great way off, . . . had compassion, and ran, and fell on his neck, and kissed him." The father didn't wait to check on the son's repentance, nor did he harass him over his sins and his wasted inheritance. The father celebrated his return and repeated this thought twice: "It was meet that we should make merry, and be glad; for this thy brother was dead, and is

alive again; and was lost, and is found." (Luke 15:11-32.)
In this parable the earthly father represented for Jesus our
heavenly Father.

Repentance is probably not necessary to gain the love
of God or Christ, but it is necessary to enable the sinner to
receive forgiveness. To feel worthy of forgiveness, we
have to recover our own integrity.

When I was a lad, a teacher brought the end of a
wooden crate, a hammer, and some nails to Sunday
School. He had each of us drive a nail into the board, to
represent one of our sins. When it was quite full, he asked
each of us to pull one out. The moral of this object lesson
was this: "You have done well to remove the nails, but
look at the damage you have done to the board. So it is
with our lives. Even though we repent," he said, "we shall
have spiritual scars forever."

This well-meaning teacher made a good point. When
we sin, we must suffer the consequences, and we hurt
others. But that is not the whole story. When we truly repent, our lives are not marred forever. Forgiveness in the
eyes of God means a clean slate, a new board. Isaiah knew
this: "Come now, and let us reason together, saith the
Lord: though your sins be as scarlet, they shall be white as
snow; though they be red like crimson, they shall be as
wool." (Isaiah 1:18.) And Ezekiel erased the slate clean
when he wrote: "But if the wicked will turn from all his
sins that he hath committed, and keep all my statutes, and
do that which is lawful and right, he shall surely live, he
shall not die. All his transgressions that he hath committed, *they shall not be mentioned unto him:* in his righteousness that he hath done he shall live. Have I any pleasure at
all that the wicked should die? saith the Lord God: and
not that he should return from his ways, and live?"
(Ezekiel 18:21-23. Italics added.)

An antidote to guilt and remorse is to make amends for
wrongdoing. Confession to those we have wronged is a
first step. This takes courage for fear of how the other person will react. Most will be reconciled quickly and will
think more of the confessor than ever. However, if the

person offended is not forgiving and gracious, that is his mistake, his sin. The sinner's responsibility is to make amends. The person wronged is responsible for his response and should be given the opportunity to grow in gospel understanding and living.

Sometimes our sins are such that we cannot make amends. If I should, through a careless act, maim or kill an innocent party, I cannot redeem a body or a life. I can, however, even in this tragic instance, confess wrongdoing and pay bills. Moreover, we all belong to one family, God's family. If I cannot repair the hurt I have done to one person, there are many others I can serve and heal just as many lives have blessed mine. If repentance can teach me compassion and lead me to suffer with and for others, in the eternal scheme of things my sins can become white as snow, though initially they were red as crimson.

The past, which we often regret, is not the rigid, fixed time span we usually conceive it to be. True, one cannot change a single event that has transpired. It is etched in life for all time. But one can change one's past as a whole. Each day we live, we add to the past, and it becomes in its totality a new thing. As the past grows, every part of it takes on new significance. A sin recently committed finds us in deep depression. Years of righteous living lift us to a higher plateau. The sin becomes a springboard to a higher sphere.

Someone has said, "Let no one till his death be called unhappy. Measure not the work until the day is out and the labor's done." Likewise, never cast one's past in concrete, for it becomes dynamic as we borrow from the future to shape and reshape the past.

One way to overcome guilt and remorse is to crowd it out and bury it with a life of constructive and joy-bringing activity. I often think that we should play the game of life with the same intensity and specificity that a basketball player plays his game. He doesn't sit back and let things happen, nor does he pine over mistakes. He is trained to do specific things—to rebound, dribble, pass, screen, shoot. Why not apply some of the same techniques to the moral life, that is, clarify values, define goals, be committed to gospel principles, keep them in sight, and practice them? And always be looking for the next chance to score, forgetting the lost ball or the bad bounce or the hasty throw.

I know a fine woman who, though not burdened with guilt, nonetheless has heavy burdens to bear. She found that constant concern neither solved her problems nor equipped her to stand up under them, so she decided to forget herself in the service of others. Several neighbors, lonely and in need of help, are now the beneficiaries of her attention and love. But it is she who has gained the most. She has learned that other people have problems too, even greater than hers. And, more important, she has felt the healing power of her own love for others. Jesus said to his disciples, speaking of a woman who had wiped his feet with her tears: "Wherefore I say unto thee, her sins, which are many, are forgiven; for she loved much." And turning to the woman, he said unto her: "Thy sins are forgiven. . . . thy faith hath saved thee; go in peace." (Luke 7:44-50.)

I had an unforgettable experience in the mission field. A brother twice my age and utterly dejected came to see me in the branch office after meeting one Sunday evening. I inquired of his trouble. He said, "Before I joined the Church, but after my marriage, I committed adultery. My wife will neither forgive me nor divorce me, and she constantly reminds me of my sin. I have come to think of myself at her estimate. My mind is confused and clouded with remorse and disgust. How," he pleaded, "can I again be pure of heart and mind?" I asked him what he had done to try to overcome his unhappy state. He replied, "Fight, fight, fight it." I suggested that there was no strength in weakness and no virtue in thinking about his sin, even in a fighting mood. So we sought other ways to help him. I prayed with and for him, and gave him a good book to read—Allan's *As a Man Thinketh, So Is He*. Finally, I asked him if he would prepare the table for the Lord's Supper in Sunday School each week. This he agreed to do despite feelings of unworthiness. Later I asked him to speak on some principle the Savior taught, which he did.

After three months he came again to my office after church and said, "Brother Bennion, I am a new man. My thoughts are what I want them to be." His simple but regular service to Jesus had changed his feeling and thinking.

I have seen others enter into a meaningful relationship with Jesus and find great strength, either not to sin or to overcome sin. Through that close relationship, they also have been assured of their forgiveness. The apostle Paul and Alma the Younger are famous as sinners who found their way to joyous and triumphant living through faith in the Lord Jesus Christ. I have also seen this in the lives of many other men and women.

Many among us have fallen into practices that go contrary to our Christian faith. Some have given up in the battle against sin. We feel unable to repent. We cannot live in constant conflict with ideals once held, so we count ourselves lost souls and seek to bury our former ideals. To such I would say two things: (1) We are all sinners. Sometimes the more "righteous" among us are guilty of sins of omission on a grand scale. This, too, God will not tolerate. No one is alone in need of repentance. (2) We may blot God out of our lives, but he will not write us off as lost souls. He is there to sustain us and help us return to old and good ways.

The tragedy of life is not to have sinned, but, having sinned, to accept defeat and henceforth to pine away our days in remorse. Matthew Cowley once said, "Man is greater than all his sins." Surely he is in the eyes of God; let him also be in his own eyes.

6

I Believe in a Positive Acceptance of Life

People have good reasons to be discouraged, pessimistic, even cynical. Personal tragedies and unsolvable social problems—illness, death, divorce, crime, poverty, and war abound on every hand. But despite the sorrows of mankind, I consider life to be a gift, a precious gift. I refuse to acknowledge defeat. Why be defeated twice, once by circumstance and once by oneself? As long as I live, I hope to face up to life with measured optimism.

Neither shall I succumb to apathy, indifference, drifting, allowing myself to be simply acted upon, pushed around by prevailing circumstances and societal norms. I admit but limited control over what happens in my world, but I do have substantial control over my response to whatever occurs. It isn't the circumstances or happenings of life that matter as much as the faith, courage, and wisdom we bring to them.

My life-affirming feeling has roots too multiple, deep, and obscure to uncover. Nevertheless, several writings and experiences have come my way that confirm and articulate this feeling.

The most realistic and least optimistic book in the Bible, Ecclesiastes, despite its emphasis on the futility of human striving ("all is vanity") recommends a positive course of action:

> Go thy way, eat thy bread with joy, and drink thy wine with a merry heart; for God now accepteth thy works.
> Let thy garments be always white; and let thy head lack no ointment.
> Live joyfully with the wife whom thou lovest all the days of the life of thy vanity, which he hath given thee under the sun, all the days of thy vanity: for that is thy portion in this life, and in thy labour which thou takest under the sun.
> Whatsoever thy hand findeth to do, do it with thy might; for there is no work, nor device, nor knowledge, nor wisdom, in the grave, whither thou goest. (Ecclesiastes 9:7-10.)

Even without faith in immortality, the author encourages us to live this life to the fullest, and this not in dissipation or despair, but joyfully with wife and work.

Dostoevsky, as a young man of twenty-eight, was condemned to be shot for his radical ideas. A few moments before the planned execution, he was told he would instead be sent to prison in Siberia. Before leaving, he was granted permission to write a letter to his brother. This was at a time when Dostoevsky had discovered his desire and power as a writer but had not yet produced his greatest novels. He wrote:

> Brother! I have not become downhearted or low-spirited. Life is everywhere life, life in ourselves, not in what is outside us. There will be people near me, and to be a man among people and remain a man for ever, not to be down hearted nor to fall in whatever misfortunes may befall me—this is life; this is the task of life. I have realized this. This idea has entered into my flesh and blood.
> Yes, it's true! The head which was creating, living with the highest life of art, which had realized the highest needs of the spirit, that head has already been cut off from shoulders. There remain the memory and images created but not yet incarnated by me. They will lacerate me, it is true. But there remains in me my heart and the same flesh and blood which can also love, and suffer, and desire, and remember, and this, after all, is life. Now, good-by, brother! Don't grieve for me!
> Live positively. There has never yet been working in me such a healthy abundance of spiritual life as now. But will my body endure? I

do not know, I am going away sick, I suffer from scrofula. But never mind, Brother, I have already gone through so much in life that now hardly anything can frighten me. Let come what may!

When I look back at the past and think how much time has been wasted in vain, how much time was lost in delusions, in errors, in idleness, in ignorance of how to live, how I did not value time, how often I sinned against my heart and spirit—my heart bleeds. Life is a gift, life is happiness, each minute might have been an age of happiness. . . . Now, changing my life, I am being reborn into a new form. Brother, I swear to you that I shall not lose hope and shall preserve my spirit and heart in purity. I shall be reborn to a better thing. This is my whole hope, my whole comfort.

Crises such as that experienced by Dostoevsky force a person to choose between acceptance and despair. Many who are not faced with dire circumstances, or who don't recognize tragedy when it occurs, drift through life lacking either vigorous acceptance or rejection. Yet there are those who, in or out of crises, by nature or nurture maintain a life-affirming attitude and live with enthusiasm and intensity.

Goethe was one such. He found life's meaning not in obtaining his goals, but in his pursuit of them. He said, "The art of living is the intensification of inborn talents." He acted from inner drives, fully aware of his action. While I do not admire all of Goethe's values, I do subscribe fully to his zest for living and his beautiful way of expressing this feeling.

In the Bhagavad Gita (Song Celestial), the devotional classic of Hinduism, I read, "To action alone hast thou a right, not to its fruits." This profound statement is consistent with Goethe's philosophy. Man proposes, life disposes. I have learned that we have but limited control over the fruit of our actions. Individuals respond to our words, intentions, and deeds from their own frame of reference, not from ours. I can control only my actions. How others respond to my ways is their business. Thus I am learning to feel, think, and act as I believe I should and to get my basic satisfaction out of my own doings. Why should I place myself at the mercy of the opinions of others?

Jesus said, "No man can serve two masters." (Matthew 6:24.) Acting to please others and myself is one way of serving two masters. Acting primarily to obtain the fruit of my actions makes of my deed a means to an end. I believe greater integrity is achieved if I act with singleness of purpose—believing my action is the right thing to do regardless of the consequences.

I find that my Mormon upbringing has contributed richly to my positive acceptance of life. Mormonism is a restoration of much of Judaism as well as Christianity. There is no original sin in the religion of Israel, but rather a rugged, realistic affirmation of earth existence marred only by man's disobedience. There are also many positive views of mortal life in the teachings of Jesus incorporated in the LDS faith. The negative aspects of Paul's teaching and the life-negation of Medieval Catholicism and of some pessimistic Protestant views of human nature have never found solid place in my view of Mormon theology. The Mormon attitude toward life is well stated in its scriptures:

> For behold, it is not meet that I should command in all things; for he that is compelled in all things, the same is a slothful and not a wise servant; wherefore he receiveth no reward.
> Verily I say, men should be anxiously engaged in a good cause, and do many things of their own free will, and bring to pass much righteousness;
> For the power is in them, wherein they are agents unto themselves. And inasmuch as men do good they shall in nowise lose their reward.
> But he that doeth not anything until he is commanded, and receiveth a commandment with doubtful heart, and keepeth it with slothfulness, the same is damned. (D&C 58:26-29.)
> Adam fell that man might be; and men are, that they might have joy. (2 Nephi 2:25.)

These passages are stated in the present tense, and they apply to earth life. In like manner, Jesus said, "I am come that they might have life, and that they might have it more abundantly." (John 10:10.) There is continuity between the temporal and the eternal. The gospel of Jesus

Christ, correctly interpreted, affirms life here and now as well as eternally.

This life-affirming attitude is not naive nor sentimental. I have observed the injustice and human suffering extant among human beings. Nazi concentration camps and contemporary terrorism are stark reminders of man's inhumanity to man. Hunger, poverty, and disease further confirm the large tragic predicament inherent in human existence. If these illustrations are not enough, we need only remember that life ends for all of us, either prematurely or in death in old age.

Recognizing all of this, I refuse to succumb to pessimism and cynicism. While I breathe and can think and act, I shall be grateful for life and shall strive to realize its value for others as well as for myself. If life were not worth living, the logical alternative would be suicide. But love of life forbids us from pursuing this path. I have learned that to enjoy living, I must accept the fact that our earthly sojourn is a struggle and a battle. But the human spirit can triumph over tragedy. With this sure knowledge, I have the great privilege to live!

In Praise of Human Nature

I rejoice in being human. I think of what man can fashion with his hands—all the things he can build, works of art he can create, instruments he can play. I love to put seeds in the ground with my hands and watch the seedlings grow, shake hands with a friend, hold hands with a child or my wife, lend a helping hand to one who is burdened with grief.

I rejoice in man's capacity to laugh and to weep. No other creature has these distinctly human qualities to any marked degree. Humor is a spice of life that helps to make its routine and tragedy bearable. Tears bear witness to compassion and empathy, and release pain that would be otherwise unbearable.

I rejoice in man's capacity to think, to organize the world about him, to give things and processes names, to establish relationships among phenomena. The world is wonderfully made; man has given meaning to his life by the power of his own thinking. He has named plants, animals, and stars. He has developed numerous and extensive symbolic systems of thought—the sciences, the arts, philosophies, religions. Think of memory! What a rich source of consciousness, not always pleasant, but always abundant.

I am particularly glad for imagination, that quality of mind that enables a person to take single images and arrange them into a mosaic that has never existed before. Without imagination there is no hope and perhaps no artistic composition or creation, little questioning, little curiosity.

As I view the whole of creation, I realize the value of man's unique gift: the ability to communicate through language—that abstract, symbolic medium of social intercourse. There are two kinds of communication, verbal and nonverbal. The verbal not only greatly broadens man's communication with others, but it also enables him to retain the heritage of the past. Language is man's tool of thought, imagination, and memory.

I rejoice in the variety of man's affective life—in the depth of his romantic feeling, the richness of his aesthetic experience, his capacity to feel deeply with other human beings. I suspect that the profundity and variety of man's emotional state follow from his having a mind to think, imagine, and remember. Whatever the explanation, feeling plays a tremendous role in human experience. From it we gain both motivation and satisfaction. The mind may guide and direct, but human drive comes largely from feeling.

I enjoy the richness and variety of human relationships. Each is unique. I appreciate the trust, loyalty, tolerance, stimulation, and openness I receive from my friends. I know what it means to be the son of a tender, unselfish, ethical father and of an uncomplaining, generous, heroic, faithful mother. I remember a quiet, stern, bearded grandfather and a grandmother who was jolly without pretense, with a warm heart and ample kitchen, a woman who stood up to life's sorrows as I do to the weather.

I know what it means to be a father of sons and daughters—to feel the pride of creation, the joy of cuddling little ones, of watching them grow in body and mind, hurting when they hurt, sharing in their moments of triumph. Each relationship is unique. A girl is a different creature from a boy, and each son gives the father a unique relationship.

There are various rewards in being a grandfather, brother to brothers, brother to sisters, nephew to uncles and aunts, cousin and double cousin. But the one human relationship that is most complete and fulfilling is that of husband and wife. It is not the easiest relationship. Because of its everydayness, intimacy, and totality, partners must work at it continually, making allowance for differences, irritations, and disagreements. Yet there is no other relationship in which two people can be so creative in both body and mind and in such a myriad of ways, no relationship in which they can know all kinds of love—romance, friendship, and Christian love—so deeply, no relationship that can endure through so many years down so many paths.

I am grateful to be a human being and a man among other human beings.

"Humanism in a Context of Faith"

Someone, I know not who, has said that "Mormonism is humanism in a context of faith." This is, in the usual meaning of these two terms, a contradiction, because humanism means that man is the measure of man, that there is nothing on earth or in heaven greater than man— neither the state nor anything supernatural. Accordingly, in humanistic philosophy, human values are the highest ones known to human beings. In the strictest terms, Mormonism cannot be called humanistic. Religious faith presupposes the supernatural, something greater than man on whom man depends and whom he holds in awe and reverence. Mormonism is such a faith.

Mormonism is humanistic, however, in the sense that it is oriented to man's life here and now as well as eternally. The Latter-day Saint faith calls for no sacrifice of present satisfactions in order to enjoy eternal values. The things that make for greatest fulfillment here will also bless us eternally. The only sacrifice demanded by the restored gospel is that of lesser values for higher ones.

While our faith looks to God for its inspiration and aspiration, it is also man-centered, revealed for the good of man. The Lord himself has declared that his "work and glory is to bring to pass the immortality and eternal life of man." (Moses 1:39.) Jesus said, "I am come that they might have life, and that they might have it more abundantly." (John 10:10.) These scriptures are spoken in the present tense. They pertain to this life. Man was not made for religion, but religion—as Jesus said of the Sabbath—was made for man.

The principles of the restored gospel are laws of life. They build the inner man; they promote fine relationships among men; they bring self-realization and fulfillment to individuals and societies that believe and practice them. I am speaking of the Ten Commandments, the Beatitudes, faith, repentance, baptism, and the gift of the Holy Spirit.

Likewise, the Word of Wisdom is a remarkable guide to present, everyday living. Not only does it promote physical health, but social and spiritual well-being as well. A Latter-day Saint who lives the Word of Wisdom well learns self-control and does not suffer the ravages of cancer and circulatory problems associated with smoking and drinking. He won't drive while drunk because he doesn't drink. He can spend his earnings on better items, if he will, than on things that destroy his body and mind.

In the same way, the Mormon concept of marriage, including chastity before and fidelity afterward, bolstered by the notion of eternity and by faith in the significance and blessing of family life, should make good marriages here and now. Temple marriages are for *time* and eternity—and unless they succeed in time, their eternal value is doubtful indeed. There is no celibacy in the Mormon idea of marriage. Man and woman were made for each other, to love one another, to be creative, and to live unselfishly but joyfully with each other and their children. A Mormon marriage can enjoy all the values of any marriage, but in addition, religious values can strengthen its meaning and the quality of its love.

The LDS faith encourages one to participate in life to the fullest, to be anxiously engaged in good causes—in play, work, church and community service, politics, school, study, and the arts. Taboo are only those things that destroy the individual—stimulants, selfishness, infidelity, materialism.

In the Mormon view, salvation is not a reward for denial of the good things of earth life for a heavenly reward. Poverty of any kind is not regarded as an asset in our spiritual well-being. Quite the contrary, salvation is a process of developing Christian character. When we die, we take much of our inner life with us into eternity—the knowledge gained, the Christian attributes acquired, the human relationships cherished. These are the ingredients of our salvation, and they simply determine our opportunities, our starting point in another sphere of life.

But Mormon emphasis on human growth and well-being here and now does not discount our need of God and Christ nor our worship of them. They remain our ideals; they are the source of our knowledge of the good life; they inspire and motivate us to live by principles that enlarge the soul; we acknowledge their boundless grace and love; they sustain us in our darkest hour. The restored gospel enables us to know the full joys of earth life, to revel in man, in his potential for good, for joy. It also leads us up the highest peaks where we can have a vision of God revealed in the life of his Son. In this sense, Mormonism is "humanism in a context of faith."

7

I Believe in Eternal Progression

One of the most distinctive and exciting teachings of the Latter-day Saints is the concept of eternal progression. The term itself is not to be found in scripture, but the idea is clearly stated in several passages, such as this: "Whatever principle of intelligence we attain unto in this life, it will rise with us in the resurrection. And if a person gains more knowledge and intelligence in this life through his diligence and obedience than another, he will have so much the advantage in the world to come." (D&C 130:18-19.)

After describing how Jesus received grace for grace until he received a fullness, a similar promise is made to his faithful disciples: "I give unto you these sayings that you may understand and know how to worship, and know what you worship, that you may come unto the Father in my name, and in due time receive of his fulness. For if you keep my commandments you shall receive of his fulness, and be glorified in me as I am in the Father; therefore, I say unto you, you shall receive grace for grace." (D&C 93: 19-20.)

Additional revelations indicate man's participation in the creative work of Deity throughout eternity. (Note D&C 76:50-70 and D&C 132.)

According to Mormon doctrine, man is not simply a creature of divine creation, but he is of the same basic nature as God. God and human beings are eternal intelligences. In addition, man is a child of God created in His image and has partaken of the divine nature. Man's need and destiny is to develop his Godlike qualities which he now experiences in an embryonic state.

This may sound blasphemous to place man in a category with God. Let me hasten to say that there is a vast difference between God's intelligence and perfection of character, and human intelligence and character. But he and we are of the same basic intelligent and moral nature. This doctrine does not debase God, but it does dignify human beings.

The purpose of this chapter is to define the concept of eternal progression and to suggest how it can be achieved.

The word *eternal* as used in scripture has two meanings, one quantitative and the other qualitative. In a quantitative sense, eternal means everlasting, without beginning or end. In this meaning of the word, we already have eternal life, for the human spirit is indestructible.

The qualitative meaning of eternal is Godlike. This is the more frequent connotation of the word eternal as used in scripture. For example, Jesus said: "And this is life eternal, that they might know thee the only true God, and Jesus Christ, whom thou has sent." (John 17:3.) Eternal life must go beyond mere immortality, or it would have no purpose.

The word *progression* also bears definition. Some people historically have had a naive faith in progression, believing that all things were improving and working toward good ends. The word simply means "the act of stepping forward," a movement toward a goal.

Progression has no value in and of itself. We can step forward to our destruction. I lost faith in progression when as a teenager I had a boil on my neck that grew and increased in discomfort. Cancer cells also grow and increase. Men progress in their potentiality to destroy the enemy in war.

The goal toward which we are striving determines the meaning and value of our progression. In gospel language, our goal is to become more like our Father in heaven as revealed in the life and character of his Son, Jesus Christ. Eternal progression is an ongoing process in which we are striving to develop divine attributes and participate in the work of Deity.

If life eternal is to know the Father and his Son, we may well ask: How can we know them? How do we get to know anyone? I think we understand others by feeling, thinking, and doing as they feel, think, and act. We understand other persons as we share the same or similar experiences. A daughter understands her own mother better after she herself gives birth to a child. A son understands his father better when he becomes a father.

This may sound presumptuous, but we can learn to know God and Christ only as we learn through experience the meaning of their attributes and participate in their "work and glory." We were created in their image. And although our divine qualities are presently in an embryonic stage of development, nevertheless they are of similar character. Deity and human beings are eternal beings of the same basic nature. The vast gap between man and Deity is not due to a difference in nature but is one of degree. Man's divinity is potential; God's is actual. Man needs an eternity to pursue and emulate the character and mind of God.

But we can progress eternally in the here and now. We can increase in our knowledge of the Father and the Son. In so doing we will fulfill the laws of our own being and will find increasing joy. To know God, we must learn and practice the attributes of Deity.

One of the hallmarks of Deity is mind or intelligence. I use the term here to mean the innate capacity to think, to know, to understand, to comprehend. God is a rational being of infinite knowledge and wisdom. He is God because of his superior intelligence. Abraham describes him as being more intelligent than all other eternal spirits: "These two facts do exist, that there are two spirits, one being more intelligent than the other; there shall be another more intelligent than they; I am the Lord thy God, I am more intelligent than they all." (Abraham 3:19.) Because of his great intelligence, God has knowledge or understanding of reality beyond the imagination of men. He also possesses supreme wisdom because he uses his knowledge in pursuit of good ends. Truly, as the Doctrine and Covenants attests, "The glory of God is intelligence." (93:36.)

Intelligence is also the glory of men and women. It distinguishes them from the rest of God's creation. In some ways, we are less than other creatures; we lack the grace and speed of a deer, the strength of a horse, the self-initiated flight of a bird. In infancy we are dependent on others for our existence much longer than other creatures. But our minds give us imagination, the capacity to create, to remember, a far richer life of feeling, and that remarkable gift—the ability to use symbols, particularly language, the tool of thought. Language enables us to build vast symbolic systems—which we call science, art, philosophy, and religion—by which we are able to interpret the world, reaching out over time and space, even to commune with God.

To cultivate the mind is one way to know God. Hence the wisdom of Proverbs:

> Get wisdom, get understanding: forget it not; neither decline from the words of my mouth.
> Forsake her not, and she shall preserve thee: love her, and she shall keep thee.
> Wisdom is the principal thing; therefore get wisdom: and with all thy getting get understanding.
> Exalt her, and she shall promote thee: she shall bring thee to honour, when thou dost embrace her.
> She shall give to thine head an ornament of grace: a crown of glory shall she deliver to thee. (Proverbs 4:5-9.)

The author of this passage, as a devout Hebrew, is admonishing us above all to learn the ways of God and to walk in his paths. (See Proverbs 3:19-26.) This is doubtless the best use of the mind we can possibly make, but it is not the only one.

If we would know God and progress eternally, we had best exercise our minds—read, think, talk ideas, study, and not spend our lives largely in pursuit of material or shallow things or in passive spectatorship of shallow, mindless radio programs, TV shows, movies, and books.

All good things—recreation, physical exercise, the comforts of life—have their place. But let us remember that mind or spirit is our uniqueness, and that things of the spirit—not externals—will go with us into eternity; they also satisfy us here, because the "kingdom of God is within" us.

One of the most often used names for Deity is Creator. The scriptures are replete with beautiful, poetic, and powerful descriptions of God's creative work. When Moses was shown some of the creations of God pertaining to this sphere, he exclaimed: "Now, for this cause I know that man is nothing, which thing I never had supposed." (Moses 1:10.) Likewise the Psalmist cried: "When I consider thy heavens, the work of thy fingers, the moon and the stars, which thou hast ordained; what is man, that thou art mindful of him, and the son of man, that thou visitest him?" (Psalm 8:3-4.) The author of Job puts man in his place as he describes the majestic creative role of God. (Job 38-41.) The Doctrine and Covenants likewise glories in the creations of Deity. (D&C 88:45-47.)

God's creative power goes beyond nature. Man himself—whether a child, a woman, or a man, whether considered aesthetically, intellectually, ethically, or spiritually—is a reflection of the Creator and bears witness to His intelligence and creativity.

If we are to progress eternally, we too must discover and use our creative powers. We must learn the joy of creation, of bringing things into being that express and reveal our nature. We need not be a Beethoven, Shakespeare, or Michelangelo, but only dare to be ourselves—to make things with our hands, to express our own thoughts, to be our honest selves and not an imitation of someone else. We can also plant gardens and grow flowers and crops, use tools to build structures, learn how to play instruments, exercise imagination, write and speak, or express whatever our talent might be. Creativity lies not so much in the end result as in the act of creation.

One way in which we can all learn to be creative, even as Jesus was in a supreme manner, is in human relations. We have the capacity to treat others with courtesy, respect, encouragement, and brotherly love, in ways that will motivate them to be their finest selves. This can be perhaps our most divine way of becoming a Creator in the image of the Lord.

Because the Nephites were walking in "straight paths," Alma knew they understood that God was a person of integrity: "I perceive that it has been made known unto you, by the testimony of his word, that he cannot walk in crooked paths; neither doth he vary from that which he hath said; neither hath he a shadow of turning from the right to the left, or from that which is right to that which is wrong; therefore, his course is one eternal round." (Alma 7:20.) Countless scriptures declare Him to be "no respecter of persons," but just, impartial and fair— a God of steadfast principles. While God is merciful and "mercy claimeth the penitent," he is never unjust. Man can depend on his impartiality. God will not deceive; he will not be fooled by flattery or deception.

If man is to know God, he too, like Job of old, must hold fast to his integrity. After trials and suffering Job could declare: "As God liveth, who hath taken away my judgment; and the Almighty, who hath vexed my soul; all the while my breath is in me, and the spirit of God is in my nostrils; my lips shall not speak wickedness, nor my tongue utter deceit. God forbid that I should justify you: till I die I will not remove mine integrity from me. My righteousness I hold fast, and will not let it go: my heart shall not reproach me so long as I live." (Job 27:2-6.)

Integrity is the mother virtue of our more personal ethical values: sincerity, humility, meekness, honesty, truthfulness, moral courage, self-control, hungering and thirsting after righteousness. All of these and more are ingredients of integrity. They help us to be one, to be whole, to feel our spiritual and inner strength. They contribute richly to our sense of freedom.

It is not easy for us to practice these virtues. We will err and stumble, but we will also increase in strength, and, as we do, we shall begin to sense—even though "through a glass darkly"—the meaning of Godhood.

John is most explicit and forceful in his description of the love of God and of our need to learn to love fellowman if we would know the Creator:

> Beloved, let us love one another: for love is of God; and every one that loveth is born of God, and knoweth God. He that loveth not knoweth not God; for God is love. . . .
>
> Herein is love, not that we loved God, but that he loved us, and sent his Son to be the propitiation for our sins. Beloved, if God so loved us, we ought also to love one another. No man hath seen God at any time. If we love one another, God dwelleth in us, and his love is perfected in us. . . .
>
> And we have known and believed the love that God hath to us. God is love; and he that dwelleth in love dwelleth in God, and God in him. Herein is our love made perfect, that we may have boldness in the day of judgment: because as he is, so are we in this world. . . .
>
> If a man say, I love God, and hateth his brother, he is a liar: for he that loveth not his brother whom he hath seen, how can he love God whom he hath not seen? And this commandment have we from him, That he who loveth God love his brother also. (1 John 4:7-8, 10-12, 16-17, 20-21.)

These verses describe much better than I can the central role love plays in the life of the Father and Son. Were their great intelligence not linked with love, I tremble to think what the universe and life would be, but man can take comfort in what many believe is God's greatest attribute—his love.

Certainly Christ, who came to earth to reveal to man the character and will of God, put love at the heart of his gospel and related all other principles to it. (See Matthew 22:36-40.) Shortly before his death, Jesus said: "A new commandment I give unto you, That ye love one another;

as I have loved you, that ye also love one another. By this
shall all men know that ye are my disciples, if ye have love
one to another." (John 13:34-35.) Surely none of us will
know God until and unless we learn to love our neighbor,
and no one, not even an atheist, will be totally without a
knowledge of the God he denies, if he truly loves his
neighbor.

To know the Father and Son, we must not only experience in some measure their attributes, but also contribute
to their work and glory—that is, assist in the development
of these same attributes in the lives of others. If we cultivate them in our own life, we will quite naturally aid
others to do likewise. Anyone who loves intelligently will
teach and encourage love in others.

Nevertheless, if we consciously serve God by serving
our fellowmen, seeking divine guidance, walking with
humility and gratitude, keeping all the commandments of
God encompassed in his great attributes, we will be more
effective as instruments in his hands.

Eternal progression is a distinctive Latter-day Saint
doctrine. It adds rich meaning to other gospel principles—to faith, repentance, forgiveness, and everlasting
life itself. It derives its basic meaning from the qualitative
meaning of the word *eternal.*

God, as revealed in Jesus Christ, is the ideal life that
we should emulate in order to realize our own divine and
human nature. As we increase in our understanding of intelligence, creativity, integrity, and love, and also seek
their realization in the lives of others, we will be pro-
gressing toward self-realization as children of God. Our
lives will be increasingly fulfilling on the path of eternal
progression, worlds without end.

8

I Believe in Increase, Growth, Improvement

After a Young Marrieds fireside, two women came to me and explained that they were near a nervous breakdown trying to do and to be all that the Church expected them to do and be. They were not seeking to rationalize their imperfections, but only to acknowledge them and their inability to carry out the admonition: "Be ye therefore perfect, even as your Father which is in heaven is perfect." (Matthew 5:48.)

The word *perfection*, if taken in its true and literal sense, means, according to Webster's unabridged dictionary, "completely accomplished, conforming completely to an absolute or a very high standard of excellence; flawless, corresponding to an actual pattern, ideal conception or archetype, pure, absolute, unmitigated, finished, consumate, fully developed." It is self-evident that no human being can in this life become completely accomplished and finished, be fully developed, or achieve an absolute state of purity. To strive for such conditions with the expectation of achieving them would be striving for the impossible.

To have God as the personification of the good life and to emulate Jesus Christ as an ideal is one thing and altogether wholesome, but to hold oneself to their state of perfection is, it seems to me, an unwise goal. Why?

The first problem we encounter in seeking ultimate perfection here and now is to know what perfection is. King Benjamin admonished his people to "believe that man doth not comprehend all the things which the Lord can comprehend." (Mosiah 4:9.) That should be obvious. We do not see as God sees, feel as he feels, think as he thinks, create as he creates, love as he loves. How can we, from our mortal perspective, fully understand the mind and character of God? Isaiah, speaking for the Creator, wisely said:

> Seek ye the Lord while he may be found, call ye upon him while he is near: Let the wicked forsake his way, and the unrighteous man his thoughts; and let him return unto the Lord, and he will have mercy upon him; and to our God, for he will abundantly pardon.
>
> For my thoughts are not your thoughts, neither are your ways my ways, saith the Lord. For as the heavens are higher than the earth, so are my ways higher than your ways, and my thoughts than your thoughts. (Isaiah 55:6-9.)

Man's idea of perfection will always be imperfect, limited by his thinking, just as it will also be an everchanging concept as he grows in his conception of God.

A second danger in pursuing our vision of absolute perfection is that it lays us open for repeated failure. Being human, we fall short of our ideals and become burdened with a sense of failure and feelings of guilt. In my experience with people in depression, it is often caused by their having set expectations that were too high for themselves and then falling short of their unrealistic goals.

A third difficulty in pursuing perfection is the chance that we might think we have succeeded. Consciousness of virtue detracts from virtue, as in the instance of the man who was proud of his humility. Virtues have their greatest meaning when they are natural and spontaneous, as in a child, and not strained, belabored, and self-conscious.

Jesus told us, in our giving of alms, to "let not thy left hand know what thy right hand doeth." (Matthew 6:3.) He had little patience with self-righteousness, as is illustrated in the following parable.

> And he spake this parable unto certain which trusted in themselves that they were righteous, and despised others:
>
> Two men went up into the temple to pray; the one a Pharisee, and the other a publican.
>
> The Pharisee stood and prayed thus with himself, God, I thank thee, that I am not as other men are, extortioners, unjust, adulterers, or even as this publican. I fast twice in the week, I give tithes of all that I possess.
>
> And the publican, standing afar off, would not lift up so much as his eyes unto heaven, but smote upon his breast, saying, God be merciful to me a sinner.
>
> I tell you, this man went down to his house justified rather than the other: for every one that exalteth himself shall be abased; and he that humbleth himself shall be exalted. (Luke 18:9-14.)

A fourth difficulty that may arise in our pursuit of perfection is undue preoccupation with self, a narrowing of life to the parameters of our own being. I once had a student, a college freshman—bright, conscientious, idealistic—whose chief concern was the perfecting of himself. He kept elaborate records in large, well-organized looseleaf notebooks of his every thought, feeling, word, and deed. In fact, he spent most of his time keeping track of himself. His life became self-centered, and quite the antithesis to the Savior's wisdom: "For whosoever will save his life shall lose it; but whosoever shall lose his life for my sake and the gospel's, the same shall find it." (Mark 8:35.)

That Jesus wanted us to set our sights high is clear. His ethical standards are lofty indeed. The commands that we love our enemy, return good for evil, and go the second mile are sufficient evidence of his idealism. But I question that he expected any of us in this life to strive for the perfection of Godhood. If we read all of scripture and various translations, we may come to a different conclusion.

In the Matthew passage, Jesus had been speaking of love. When he said "Be ye therefore perfect," he may have had in mind that we should be perfect in love as an ideal. A student of mine, Allen Price, pointed that out to me some thirty years ago.

In Luke, the Sermon on the Mount is scattered, not of one piece. And the author writes: "Be ye therefore merciful, as your Father also is merciful." (Luke 6:36.) In the New English Bible, Matthew 5:48 reads: "There must be no limit to your goodness, as your Heavenly Father's goodness knows no bounds."

In place of striving for absolute perfection, I suggest that it is wiser and far more fruitful to strive for improvement, to try to become converted and live gospel principles with joy. Innumerable scriptures call for us to increase in virtue.

Jesus himself "increased in wisdom and stature, and in favour with God and man." (Luke 2:52.) In his ministry he declined the title "Good Master" from a disciple and said: "Why callest thou me good? there is none good but one, that is, God." (Mark 10:18.) Jesus received not the fullness at first, but received grace for grace. (D&C 93:12.) His perfection, the fullness of grace, doubtless came to him after his triumphant mission was completed.

In his teaching, Christ stressed our need for growth and increase. His was a call to repentance, a plea for action: "Ask, and it shall be given you; seek, and ye shall find; knock, and it shall be opened unto you." (Matthew 7:7.) Likewise, his disciples, Peter and Paul, recognized our need for growth and encouraged it:

> As newborn babes, desire the sincere milk of the word, that ye may grow thereby; if so be ye have tasted that the Lord is gracious. (1 Peter 2:2-3.)
> But grow in grace, and in the knowledge of our Lord and Saviour Jesus Christ. (2 Peter 3:18.)
> And beside this, giving all diligence, add to your faith virtue; and to virtue knowledge; and to knowledge temperance; and to temperance patience; and to patience godliness; and to godliness brotherly kindness; and to brotherly kindness charity. For if these things be in you, and abound, they make you that ye shall neither be barren nor unfruitful in the knowledge of our Lord Jesus Christ. (2 Peter 1:5-8.)

The apostle Paul, conscious of his own limitations and the foibles of men, was quick to acknowledge the limits of our knowledge and virtue: "And if any man think that he knoweth anything, he knoweth nothing yet as he ought to know." (1 Corinthians 8:2.) "For we know in part, and we prophesy in part. . . . For now we see through a glass, darkly; but then face to face: now I know in part; but then shall I know even as also I am known." (1 Corinthians 13:9, 12.)

I am in full sympathy with the notion that we should "hitch our wagon to a star." We should not be content with mediocrity, passivity, stagnation. The religious life is a call to be born again, to find a new spirit, to live adventurously for high ideals and for great causes. But to return to the problem of the two women that initiated this discussion, there is no necessity to become frustrated in the pursuit of faith and righteousness. The gospel, in the words of James, is the law of liberty. (James 1:25; 2:12.) In the words of Jesus, it is to become free: "Ye shall know the truth, and the truth shall make you free." (John 8:32.)

The way to find joy and freedom in gospel living is not to strive for the perfection of Deity here and now. Such a goal is immodest and impossible. Rather, let us become converted to the ideals the Savior taught; let us fall in love with them and not be afraid to live by them. Let us hunger and thirst after his righteousness—serve God and man with singleness of purpose, with purity of motive, with a glad heart. Let us establish goals, patterns of behavior, and traditions consistent with the character and will of God. Then spiritual growth will come as a by-product of spiritual living, and we shall be moving in the direction of our Savior's divine life. In place of stress and self-concern will come the fruit of gospel living described by Alma: "And because of your diligence and your faith and your patience with the word in nourishing it, that it may take root in you, behold, by and by ye shall pluck the fruit thereof, which is most precious, which is sweet above all that is sweet, and which is white above all that is white, yea, and pure above all that is pure; and ye shall feast upon this fruit even until ye are filled, that ye hunger not, neither shall ye thirst." (Alma 32:42.)

9

I Believe in Brotherhood

I grew up in a Christian home. My father was a world citizen of the highest type. I can remember no expressions of prejudice or acts of discrimination toward ethnic groups in my parents' home. Nor do I recall ever feeling any malice or disdain toward any minority group. My sin, rather, was indifference, lack of sensitivity to the feelings of others. My friends and I recited "eeny meeny miny mo . . . ," took part in minstrel shows mimicking, as we thought, Negroes. We called Chinese "Chinks," and Japanese "Japs." Even Eastern and Southern Europeans were not considered quite the equal of those of us born of British stock. The name Dago for Italians was commonly spoken, and Germans were Huns in World War I, a fearsome people. Jews were stereotyped by a brand of jokes.

Out on Highland Drive in Salt Lake City stood an eating house where we could buy a chicken sandwich and rootbeer after a show. Its name: Coon Chicken Inn. A huge caricature of a black man served as a name and sign, his open mouth as a doorway. It never occurred to me in those years to be angry or ashamed of that indignity toward blacks.

At twenty, I went on a mission to Germany and lived with wonderful German Saints. It was during the depression of the 1930s, and they shared their only good meal of the week with us. I partook of their hospitality and learned much from them of humility and faith. Not only that, I also observed their neatly cared-for gardens, parks, and cities, listened to the music of Beethoven and Wagner, read something of Schiller, Goethe, and Kant, and was the recipient of honest and solid workmanship in every facet of living. Any prejudice toward Germans I had entertained soon vanished. I came to love their vigor, industry, tidiness, music, idealism, language, openness.

At the University of Strasbourg, I became friendly with a Hindu from India. He was nearly as dark as our proverbial "ace of spades," and as gentle and spiritual a person as one could meet. I asked him what he thought of European life. He replied: "I was never so shocked, coming to Switzerland after reading the New Testament. I saw no resemblance, no reflection of the gospel in the lives of the people." I wonder what he would have thought had he come to a country less clean and more commercialized than Switzerland.

This Hindu friend, a student of medicine, lived the Mormon Word of Wisdom in its prohibitions and refrained also from eating eggs and meat. I asked him why. He answered, "So my mind can rule my body." He may not have been physiologically sound in his diet, but his motivation was remarkable and inspiring.

That same year in Strasbourg, having become friends with a man from the French-speaking part of Switzerland, I invited him and his wife to our apartment for supper. He brought a tall, queenly black woman from Morocco whom he had married while he was working as a civil servant in that French colony. After supper she was admiring our blue-eyed, red-haired, rosy-cheeked baby daughter. Tears flowed freely down her cheeks as she showed love and affection for our child. In response to my question of concern, she remarked that she had been married seven years and longed for a baby. I lost much of my prejudice toward blacks—which carried over from my childhood—that evening as I observed her modest, humble, yet gracious and lovely manner toward our baby.

Early in my years of teaching at the institute of religion at the University of Utah, a black woman of forty-five joined my Mormon Doctrine class. She was a daughter of a Protestant minister in Ogden, Utah, and had come to the university hoping to study social work, but had been rejected because of low grades. I asked her one day after class why she came to my class in Mormon theology. She answered: "In the summertime, I'm a recreation leader on a playground in Ogden. Half of the children are white, mostly Latter-day Saints. They come to me with all kinds of questions. I have come to learn of your religion, so that when I answer them I will not hurt their faith."

I am amazed and chagrined that it has taken me a lifetime to come to a profound appreciation for people of all races. I have come to appreciate the words of Paul: "There is neither Jew nor Greek, there is neither bond nor free, there is neither male nor female: for ye are all one in Christ Jesus. . . . For in Jesus Christ neither circumcision availeth any thing, nor uncircumcision; but faith which worketh by love." (Galatians 3:28; 5:6.) And of Nephi: "And he inviteth them all to come unto him and partake of his goodness; and he denieth none that come unto him, black and white, bond and free, male and female; and he remembereth the heathen; and all are alike unto God, both Jew and Gentile." (2 Nephi 26:33.) "And the one being is as precious in his sight as another." (Jacob 2:21.)

Human beings are not equal in their native intelligence, artistic potential, anticipated longevity, or opportunities in life, but they are equal in their basic need for food, warmth, love, self-respect, creative self-expression, and response from other human beings. They are equal in their need for self-fulfillment and salvation.

Human beings are equal in that they were all created in the image of God; all have partaken of the divine nature. As children of God, we must all learn to love and create and be free, if we would fulfill the measure of our

creation. Limitations of the body, heredity, and environment becloud our vision of what lies hidden in every
human being. But in God's due time and, we hope too,
with our increasing concern for fellowman, all people will
be given the opportunity to come into their own and be
what God and nature intended they should be.

Human beings are equal as recipients of the love of
God because his love is unconditional, unmerited, impartial, and universal. God loves the sinner as much as the
saint. This is beautifully illustrated in the life of Jesus, who
gave special concern to the outcasts of Jewish society—
sinners and publicans. He came to heal the sick among
men; the well, he said, need no physician. Christ died for
Chicanos as well as for Anglos, for blacks as well as for
Caucasians. All are God's children.

How long will it be before we will look beyond skin
and even beyond culture and see in every human being a
child of God and a brother or sister with the same fears,
hungers, longings, needs, and joys that each of us has?
How long will it be before we learn that God is no respecter of persons, that he has no favorites, that all are
alike and equally sacred before him? How long will it take
us to learn that to be a chosen people means simply to
have the responsibility of serving our fellowmen for God?
How long before we learn that what God has given to us,
we should use to bless our neighbors?

I shall never again—God help me—judge a man by
the color of his skin, nor will I demean a fellow being by
labeling him inferior as a person. There is a quality of
goodness and greatness and sacredness in every child of
God. I will never write one off. He is my brother; she is my
sister—flesh of my flesh, spirit of my spirit.

10

I Believe in Setting Loyalties in Religion

Being religious can mean many different things, like going to church, reading scripture, believing in God, keeping the commandments. In fact, religion embraces so much that one needs to cast his own religious beliefs and feelings into some kind of mold or framework that will bring simplicity out of complexity and order out of miscellany.

There is, of course, more than one acceptable way to integrate one's religious living into a meaningful whole. I wish to do so in terms of three basic loyalties. One reason for my choice is that if the religious life means commitment, then it appears logical to think of it in terms of loyalties. I write in personal terms; I cannot speak for anyone else, since I am not sure others share these same commitments in the order in which I do, if at all.

My first, central, and highest loyalty is to persons, both mortal and divine. Nothing else in religion, on earth or in the universe, is quite as important. Nothing matters ultimately as much as what happens to persons and relationships between persons.

Many experiences and ideas have led me to this con-
viction, including religion itself. Nothing inspires me
more than the view of creation depicted in the first chapter of Moses (verse 39) in which the prophet is given a
glimpse of some of the creations of God through the Son
and is told that "worlds without number have I created."
Moses pressed his Creator to tell him the meaning of his
endless, ongoing creations. Finally, the now well-known
answer came: "For behold, this is my work and my glory—
to bring to pass the immortality and eternal life of man."
(Moses 1:39.)

It would seem that "eternal" in this context has a qualitative connotation, meaning Godlike, even as it does in
the Gospel of John, wherein Christ said, "This is life eternal, that they might know thee the only true God, and
Jesus Christ, whom thou hast sent." The very work of
Deity is to bring all of mankind to a greater realization of
the life that God knows, to help men increase in integrity,
love, freedom, and creativity, to achieve the full measure
of their creation as children of God. If this is the divine
purpose, why should it not become yours and mine, if we
are to do God's will and love him with all our hearts,
minds, and souls?

The Hebrew prophets have taught me in unforgettable
language to care above all else for what happens to persons. In the days of Amos, ancient Israel was doing many
things in the name of religion—keeping the sabbath and
the new moon, offering sacrifices, uttering prayers, re-
membering their fathers, Abraham, Isaac, and Jacob. But
they had forgotten one thing—God's concern for man. To
paraphrase Amos, they were at ease in Zion, playing musi-
cal instruments, drinking wine out of bowls, stretching
themselves in idle luxury as the chosen of God, but they
were "not grieved for the affliction of Joseph." (See Amos
6:1-6.) They gave no thought to the widow, the orphan,
the poor, those who were "hurting," except to sell them
into slavery for the price of a pair of shoes or to take advantage of them in the court by bribes and deception.

Among the prophets, Micah defined religion most

beautifully when he asked and then answered his own question: "Wherewith shall I come before the Lord, and bow myself before the high God?" Not, he continues, with sacrifices and rivers of oil and human sacrifice, for "He hath showed thee, O man, what is good; and what doth the Lord require of thee, *but to do justly, and to love mercy, and to walk humbly with thy God?*" (Micah 6:6-8. Italics added.) Here Micah is defining religion in terms of personal relationships between man and man (do justly and love mercy) and between man and God (walk humbly).

You are familiar with the Savior's concern for persons. He had, I believe, two supreme loyalties—to his Father and to his fellowmen. He began his ministry by quoting from Isaiah: "The Spirit of the Lord is upon me, because he hath anointed me to preach the gospel to the poor; he hath sent me to heal the brokenhearted, to preach deliverance to the captives, and recovering of sight to the blind, to set at liberty them that are bruised." (Luke 4:18.) Follow the Christ through the Gospels, and you will see how closely he kept to his original charge. "He went about doing good." Even sinners "drew near unto him." He sought out those who needed him, fed their hunger and stilled their thirst. Even the sacred law—the Sabbath—in his eyes was made for man. "Is it lawful . . . to do good, or to do evil? to save life, or to destroy it?" was the question that guided his actions. (Luke 6:9.) Christ was as humane and man-centered as any humanist in his concern for persons, and he also loved God and shared with him his love for man.

And so my loyalty to persons includes man, every man, I hope, but also Deity—the Father and the Son. They too are persons. I don't know that they need my direct adoration and affection, but it's my simple faith that they suffer when men suffer and rejoice when men have cause to rejoice. So in a modest way, but with all my heart, I would diminish their suffering and enhance their joy.

My second loyalty in religion is to the principles of the gospel: to faith, repentance, justice, freedom, love and its many expressions—empathy, mercy, and forgiveness.

These have my loyalty because I have seen what they do for persons, how they help them to be whole, hopeful, self-controlled, and generous; how they refine and enrich human relationships and increase peace and good will among men.

I have seen these principles work in the lives of converts, countless students, and friends. One young man confessed that he had committed every sin in the book: stealing, adultery, drunkenness, and hypocrisy. Then I saw him find faith in Christ and overcome greed and lust and regain self-respect, a self-respect chastened by "the furnace of affliction," mellowed and meek but not without strength and joy. There comes to mind also a young woman, single and alone, who was once steeped in fear and self-pity. I heard her say, "I used to be afraid of life and of myself, but I am afraid no more. I can love and serve others. I have found joy in following the Master."

Gospel principles do not excite me in the abstract. They have meaning only in the life of the individual and in his relationship to fellowman and Deity. And so my second loyalty is intimately related to the first.

This, too, I have learned from Jesus. He was not committed to the law as an end, but used it to serve life. His entire mission was geared to human needs: he taught repentance, not to the righteous but to sinners, and gave hope to the poor, the healing power of faith to the afflicted, and forgiveness to sinners. Gospel principles and human need were inseparable in his mind.

To be a disciple of Christ, one doesn't always have to be turning the other cheek. Christ knocked over the tables of money changers, called Herod "that old fox," and told Peter, "Get thee behind me, Satan." He called principles into play to effect change in human life and behavior. We too can use gospel principles in business, in politics, in the courthouse, and in the classroom. There are some appropriate to every situation.

My *third loyalty in religion is to the Church.* I place it third, not because it is unimportant, but because, in my judgment, it is instrumental to the other two loyalties already discussed. In the language of Paul, Christ "gave some, apostles; and some, prophets; . . . for the perfecting of the saints, . . . till we all come in the unity of the faith, and of the knowledge of the Son of God, unto a perfect man, unto the measure of the stature of the fulness of Christ: that we . . . speaking the truth in love, may grow up into him in all things." (Ephesians 4:11-15.) The Church is not an end to be served, but an instrument through which together we may serve God and man. It is a fellowship, called and ordained of the Lord, blessed and empowered from on high, to inculcate the principles and spirit of the gospel into the lives of men.

I am grateful to the Church, for within its fold I have begun to learn and experience the meaning of the gospel. In it I have found a choice fellowship with co-believers; through it I have received faith, the gift of the Holy Spirit, the priesthood, and rich opportunities of service and worship.

But again, one cannot serve in the Church fruitfully without prior loyalties to God and man. I once asked a group of Church workers: "What is your goal in your position in the Church?" A coach of an M-Men basketball team answered, "To win the stake and, if possible, the Church championship." I asked, "Is this your first and highest purpose as a coach?" He replied, "Yes." How misguided! With such a goal one might lie, cheat, play unfair, and ignore the inner life of any or every person on the squad. Even in basketball, one's first commitment ought to be to the players and his second to principles of fair play, brotherhood, honest effort. Winning should be at most only the means to human ends.

In organized religion there is always the danger that institutional ends become the goals of religion. Meetings may be held as ends in themselves, missionary work measured in terms of baptismal quotas, and welfare projects evaluated in quantitative terms. When this happens, the religious life becomes idolatrous—serving false gods instead of God and his children. Whenever institutional goals are placed first, persons become means to these ends, and integrity and love become secondary, if not forgotten.

Years ago I learned of a scoutmaster who, eager to have 100 percent of his boys advanced at honor night, promised the only one who had not earned an award that he would let him pass his test the following week, if he would only show up for honors on the award night. Fortunately, the boy refused to go along with his scoutmaster.

A thing like this may happen because the Church, though called of God, is made up of people like you and me, among whom "many are called but few are chosen," and our human interests and ambitions becloud our vision of God's work and glory, "to bring to pass the immortality and eternal life of man."

Yes, I have three basic loyalties in religion: *to persons, to gospel principles, and to the Church.* They are not in conflict with one another, but blend beautifully even as the moon, stars, and open sky, *if* I remember all three and serve each in proper relation with the others.

11

I Believe in Harmony Between Social Science and Religion

Early in this century W. I. Thomas, an American sociologist, made a study of five hundred girls who were in trouble to ascertain the reasons for their social maladjustment. He concluded that their difficulties resulted from the fact that their basic psychological needs were not fulfilled. These were, in his judgment, security, new experience, recognition, and response.

By security, he meant affectional security. The girls were not loved; they lacked warm affectional ties. By new experience he meant just the opposite of security. Persons crave adventure, excitement, creativity. They are born to function, to be free. By recognition, the sociologist meant self-recognition. A person must find his identity, feel his own worth, accept himself or herself. Finally, by response, he meant that persons cannot tolerate apathy and indifference. They crave reaction, response to their feelings, ideas, actions.

Psychologists, psychiatrists, social workers, and other students of human behavior are in substantial agreement about man's essential psychological needs and of their great significance in people's lives, even though each professional may use his own peculiar nomenclature to describe these needs.

In my terminology, man's primary psychological needs are: (1) to give and receive love, (2) to express oneself creatively, and (3) to have a feeling of self-acceptance and worth. These needs overlap and reinforce each other. A person who is creative gains self-esteem. A person who is loved also feels his own worth heightened. Feeling his own worth, he is free to love.

Religion, especially as taught and lived by Jesus, recognizes these basic human desires and needs and, when understood and practiced, goes a long way toward their fulfillment. Let me illustrate.

1. The social scientist speaks of affectional security, belongingness, acceptance by significant others. Jesus speaks of love—a love that is alter-ego-centered, unconditional, unmerited, universal, large enough to include even one's enemy.

Jesus exemplified this loving acceptance of others, particularly those thought to be the "lowest" of human beings: sinners, publicans, beggars, lepers. He mingled freely with rich and poor. "Then drew near unto him the publicans and sinners for to hear him." (Luke 15:1.) He made love the central principle of his gospel, the one on which every other principle depends. Without love, no action is efficacious. The apostle Paul caught the essence of Christ's teaching when he wrote: "And though I have the gift of prophecy, and understand all mysteries, and all knowledge, and though I have all faith, so that I could remove mountains, and have not charity, I am nothing." (1 Corinthians 13:2. Read the whole chapter!) I know no one who has taught and lived the principle of love as effectively as Jesus of Nazareth.

2. Behavioral scientists speak of man's need for new experience, for freedom of self-expression; religion speaks of free agency. There is a tendency in organized religion to restrict man's freedom, to burden him with norms and commandments that restrict and narrow his vision. This is

not so in the teachings of Jesus and the Hebrew prophets. These men were revolutionary. They broke with many traditional practices and patterns of thinking. Jesus said, "it is written, . . . but I say unto you" or "It hath been said, . . . but I say unto you." He freed men from the burden of the Sabbath and made it a day to heal, to save life, to glorify God.

Religion teaches that man is in the image of God. Since God is the great Creator, man cannot satisfy his nature unless he, too, becomes a creator in his own right and sphere. He must view religion as an opportunity more than as a possession—an opportunity to love, to serve, to walk boldly by faith in the great ideals of his religion. The Christian faith is, in the words of Paul, a call to liberty.

3. Behavioral scientists have recognized man's need to feel his own self-worth. Jesus had a profound regard for persons. They were more important to him than even the law of God as revealed through Moses. Man was not made for the Sabbath, but the Sabbath was made for man. Man was not made to glorify the law, but the law was there to elevate man. On several occasions Jesus invoked forgiveness or mercy when, in the eyes of others, the law called for punishment. The woman caught in adultery, according to the law, should have been stoned. Jesus sent her on her way with the gracious words, "Neither do I condemn thee: go, and sin no more." (John 8:11.)

He taught men nearly two thousand years ago not to be judgmental. "Judge not, that ye be not judged." And "why beholdest thou the mote that is in thy brother's eye, but considerest not the beam that is in thine own eye?" (Matthew 7:1, 3.)

Jesus took simple fishermen and made spiritual giants of them. He imbued them with belief in the worth of souls, making them fishers of men.

In his heart there was room for rich and poor, sinner and saint, children, the afflicted, the hungry, even those who lifted him up on the cross. He had tolerance for everyone, it would appear, except hypocrites and the self-righteous. He spoke harshly to them, but his rebuke may have been in their interest and born of love. No one else, to my knowledge, has treated human beings with quite the respect and love in word and deed as did Jesus of Nazareth.

4. Behavioral scientists speak of man's need for response. In modern terminology this means communication both verbal and nonverbal. Man cannot survive in isolation; he suffers under indifference and apathy.

The gospel of Jesus Christ is a social gospel. It teaches man to seek out the widow, the orphan, the afflicted, the poor, the sinner, those who mourn. The very word *religion* means to bind together. The Christian church was established as a community of believers who would meet together the first day of the week and eat a common meal in remembrance of the founder of their faith. They had all things in common. They sang and prayed together and taught one another. One of the major values of religion is to provide the bonds of brotherhood to every human being who will accept the same. Other ties are broken by death, divorce, graduation, and change of employment and location, but the church—the congregation—is always there to communicate with the individual.

In religion there is not only response between persons, but also between human beings and the God they worship. People are isolated in the universe traveling through space on this earth-ship. Through faith they can feel themselves part of total being. Jesus taught men to pray unto the Father and to trust in his goodness.

Behavioral scientists and religionists, it seems to me, are in fundamental agreement concerning man's basic psychological needs. Their respective criticisms of each other lie elsewhere, and often where either one—in the opinion of the other—violates human nature.

When scientists and religionists place persons and human values central and uppermost, their respective efforts draw closer together and harmonize, although their terminology and methods vary. The religionist, for example, speaks of repentance, whereas the counselor encourages his client to face up to reality and accept responsibility for his actions. Thus, both scientist and religionist recognize man's need to achieve greater integrity.

In this complex, urban society, human beings have great difficulty in satisfying their basic psychological needs. They need all the understanding and help both the behavioral sciences and religion can provide in order to find fulfillment. Social scientists and religionists would do well to respect each other's approach—so long as it is meeting man's need for love, creative self-expression, feelings of self-worth, and feelings of being at home among men and in the universe.

12

I Believe in the Logic
of the Gospel

Some people delight in pitting faith against reason, and thereby disparage thinking in order to exalt religion. They even find scriptural justification for taking this stance in the writings of Paul, particularly in the early chapters of First Corinthians. The apostle knew from experience that the learned Greeks in Athens were not disposed to believe his account of the resurrected Christ. It was therefore easy for him to declare that "the wisdom of this world is foolishness with God." (1 Corinthians 3:19.)

When one depreciates the thinking of men, he may also unwittingly demean thinking within religion itself and run the risk of practicing a form of religion that is a mixture of feeling, tradition, recollection, hearsay, and opinion—a kind of conglomerate with limited substance and structure.

Let me hasten to say that I do not disparage faith. Religion deals with the unknown, with superempirical reality, with ultimate questions that in good part, transcend experience and logic. It must, therefore, go beyond knowledge in its quest for meaning and the ideal. Nor do I deny Paul's statement "that the things of God knoweth no man, but the Spirit of God." (1 Corinthians 2:11.) Revelation is more than man's thinking; it is the Spirit of God working on and through the mind of man.

Granted all of that, this does not mean that a religious person must set aside reason, close his eyes to thought, and cease being rational when he practices his religion. Thinking is fruitful not just in science, philosophy, art, and everyday life; it is equally so within religion itself. The gospel of Jesus Christ is more than feeling, more than hope, more than faith. It is also built upon ideas. It has an inner logic that infers a use of the mind in order for one to understand and appreciate it.

The teachings of Jesus reveal a person of faith, a mystic in the finest sense of the word who spoke of the ultimate, his God, in the most trustful words, a person of deep feeling and sensitivity. But they also bear witness to a lucid, brilliant mind. His parables are profound and artistic; his proverbs meaty, pithy, and insightful; his questions and answers incisive. His ideas hang together, support each other, show consistency, and form configurations of meaning not unlike the coherence one finds in philosophy and science, howbeit of a different kind.

His major appeal to men is that they should love one another. His life and teachings are wholly consistent with this emphasis: "It is more blessed to give than to receive"; "Judge not, that ye be not judged"; "Blessed are the merciful" and "the peacemakers"; "He that would save his life, shall lose it"; "If a man ask thee to go one mile, go with him twain"; "Forgive seventy times seven." In fact, everything in the law and the prophets hangs on this principle of love.

The second moral virtue Jesus stressed and exemplified is integrity. This ideal embraces all of the moral virtues of the gospel that are not preempted by love, the mother of the social virtues. Sincerity, humility, meekness, hunger and thirst after righteousness, absence of pretense and guile, repentance, freedom, and moral courage are all ingredients and expressions of integrity, of which Jesus spoke abundantly.

Integrity and love, coupled together, build the moral life of the Christian. The gospel of Jesus Christ, in its moral dimension, provides a thoughtful framework built on these two principles and made real in the life of its author. These virtues challenge the mind as well as the heart.

H. C. King, in his *Ethics of Jesus,* points out the inner logic of the Beatitudes. He calls them a map of life and shows how each builds on and presupposes those that have gone before. The first four are more personal and, in my view, are expressions of integrity. Living these prepares one to express love as illustrated in the second group of four. A summary of King's view of the meaning of the Beatitudes is as follows:

1. The poor in spirit = those who are humble, who feel their spiritual need.

2. They who mourn = those who are penitent, who recognize their sins and mistakes and correct them.

3. The meek = those who have self-control, who are free from the necessity of guarding the self.

4. They who hunger and thirst after righteousness = those who practice integrity, who seek the highest good.

5. The merciful = those who are sympathetic, compassionate.

6. The pure in heart = those who are guileless, selfless.

7. The peacemakers = those who promote love among men.

8. The persecuted for righteousness' sake = those who sacrifice for others.

The Beatitudes are not simply a miscellaneous statement of beautiful sayings—they are an integrated work of thoughtful reflection. Like steps on a ladder, they lead from one to another upward.

Just as there is consistency among the ethical teachings of the gospel, so there is also a relatedness and coherence within its theological and worshipful aspects. For example, the first principles and ordinances of the gospel are not separate ideas and practices, but, like the Beatitudes, they build on each other and form a meaningful whole. Faith in Christ leads naturally to repentance, which means acquiring a new mind. Baptism is a meaningful symbolic witness of one's repentance and search for a new life as a disciple of Christ. And when one is stirred by faith, has been made more whole and contrite by repentance, and has entered the fellowship of cobelievers, he is ready to receive the Holy Ghost, who will fill his life with "perfect love." Partaking of the Lord's Supper is a meaningful way of renewing this process of becoming a disciple of Jesus.

Modern scriptures, even as the Bible, were not written as theological texts. And Mormonism has not yet been developed into a completely consistent, comprehensive theology. Maybe it never should be, because theology tends to become abstract and sterile compared to the spontaneous preaching and writing of the prophets. Yet there are many groupings of ideas within the restored gospel that have appeal because they cohere logically and suggest rational solutions to vital issues. Space will permit only one or two illustrations.

Latter-day Saint teachings concerning the eternal, uncreated nature of man's intelligence, the elements, laws, and time and space suggest important implications for the problems of human freedom and the presence of so much natural and moral evil—two of the most difficult problems of theology. If, as in traditional, historical Christianity, God is conceived as being omnipotent and omniscient and the ultimate source of all creation, it is most difficult to see how man as his total creature is free in relation to the Creator. It is also most difficult to square the gross amount of human suffering, injustice, and inequality with the goodness of God. By contrast, in Mormon thought, free agency is an eternal aspect of man's uncreated intelligence and is God-protected and respected rather than God-given in an ultimate sense. In Mormon doctrine, much of natural evil may logically follow from the eternal elements and laws with which the Creator must work, and moral evil is the result of man's inhumanity to man.

This Mormon philosophy of eternalism and spiritual pluralism raises other questions, as any theological system does, but it has great meaning for the religious life. It makes faith, repentance, personal responsibility for self and others, and the whole moral and religious life real, without in any way depreciating God as the ideal or his abundant grace as essential elements in the gospel plan.

There are other configurations of ideas within Mormon thought that have consistency and that appeal to the mind. For example, the Mormon idea of a very personal concept of Deity goes well with the belief in continuous revelation, the production of new scripture, the fatherhood of God, and the eternal progression of man toward the eternal character and creativity of God and Christ.

If I have been able thus far to suggest the considerable degree of rationality in the gospel, then it must follow that anyone who believes in and practices the gospel would profit by thinking as well as by feeling. As Jesus said, one should love God with all his mind as well as with all his heart. May I suggest two ways in which one can and ought to use his mind in his religious life.

1. One ought not (in the words of Levi Edgar Young) to pulverize the gospel, live it piecemeal, one rule or principle at a time bolstered by a single text. It is more prudent to keep in mind the gospel as a whole, a framework of fundamental principles, to which lesser and single ideas can be related and from which they receive their meaning. For example, Latter-day Saints believe in the fatherhood, justice, love, and intelligence of God. Believing this, I do not accept interpretations of his character or ways that contradict his impartiality, love, or intelligence. Everything that men have said and done in the name of God cannot be accepted at face value unless it is consistent with his character and purpose. And for me, Jesus Christ best reveals the character, spirit, and will of God. What I

cannot square with Christ's teachings, I will question no matter what the source. The nature of God then becomes a basic, rational guide with which to interpret the religious and moral life. This, in my judgment, is the most significant purpose of theologizing.

Another example of using a grouping of ideas as a guide in the religious life is found in the Mormon doctrine of man. We believe that man is eternal, created in the image of God, with capacity for freedom and with responsibility for himself and others; that all men are brothers and have the capacity to grow in the likeness of God; that all may share increasingly in God's creative work and glory, and find joy by fulfilling their human and divine natures. Believing this, I refuse to accept any interpretation of scripture or of the gospel that contradicts or impedes the free agency of man and his brotherhood with all men, or that bars his opportunity for self-realization.

2. Another way to exercise reason in the religious life is in its application to the practical aspects of living. Man has learned a good deal about the universe through astronomy and physics, about nature through chemistry and biology, and about the mind and society through the behavioral-social sciences, although admittedly there is less agreement in the sciences that study human behavior. If religion is to find its full and rightful place in human experience, it must relate to the knowledge and wisdom of human experience. The Word of Wisdom and the sciences of health and nutrition need each other. The Christian principles of integrity and love are consistent with and supplemental to the knowledge of human nature born of scientific study.

In summary, religion is more than feeling, more than hope, more than mystery. It also includes moral precepts and theological postulates that provide thoughtful perspectives on significant areas of life. The religious life should be motivated by faith, but also be guided by the logic of the gospel as well as by the Spirit. I believe that impressions of the Spirit should be checked by the logic of gospel fundamentals even as I believe we should pray concerning our rational conclusions. I find it distasteful and inappropriate to hear people disparage reason in order to glorify God. If the glory of God is intelligence, then intelligence is no less the glory of man, who was created in His image. Jacob said it well to those who believe: "But to be learned is good if they hearken unto the counsels of God." (2 Nephi 9:29.)

13

I Believe That to Be a Mormon, I Must Be Christian

We Mormons are considered by others and by ourselves as a separate and distinctive people. From the beginning of our history, we have never quite fit into the larger American society. Like the Jews, albeit for a much shorter period, we have stood apart. Like them, we have had trouble with our neighbors, having been driven from place to place and harassed for our beliefs and practices.

Brigham Young and his followers sought to build a kingdom of their own in the West—an ambition that was eventually thwarted by the coming of Johnston's army in 1858 and the antipolygamy pressures and raids from 1862 to 1890. When the "wars" were over, Utah proudly became a state in 1896 and joined the union, but the Mormons have remained an uncommon people in the eyes of others and a distinctive people in their own. Today, we are still a subculture within a national culture, absorbed but yet not assimilated.

Latter-day Saints, at least the believing and more active ones, marry within the faith for time and eternity, do genealogy and temple work, pay tithing, work on welfare farms, store food for emergencies, hold Monday night family home evenings, go on unpaid proselyting missions, do not smoke or drink or use other harmful substances, read their own scriptures along with the Bible, follow a living prophet, and believe in divine authority and the uniqueness of their calling as custodians of the gospel of Jesus Christ.

Non-Mormons recognize some of these unusual features, so much so that I have been asked more than once, "Are Mormons Christians? I never see the cross on your churches nor hear the word *grace* in your sermons. I see no distinctive Christian architecture." Many think of Mormonism not as one of the Christian movements, but rather as a people with a pioneer tradition, a work ethic, a practical people meeting their own needs.

Of greater interest to me than how others view us, however, is how we think of ourselves. How would a Latter-day Saint finish the sentence, "A Latter-day Saint is a person who . . ."? I have tried lately to get at the self-perceptions of youthful members of the Church by asking two questions without warning. First I ask, "What *don't* you do because you're a Latter-day Saint?" The answers are:

> I don't smoke.
> I don't drink.
> I don't carouse.
> I don't go to movies on Sunday.
> I don't profane the name of God.

Then I ask, "What *do* you do because you are a Latter-day Saint?" The answers begin:

> I go to Sunday School.
> I go to priesthood meetings.
> I go to sacrament meeting.
> I go to seminary.
> I pay tithing.
> I plan to go on a mission.
> I will be married in the temple.

In short, when caught off guard and responding extemporaneously, LDS youth stress things peculiar to their faith. In no way do I wish to discredit this. I am profoundly grateful for the Word of Wisdom. I attend meetings. I believe in the principle of tithing. I went on a mission and appreciate that opportunity. However, these practices are not the heart of the life of a true Latter-day Saint, but are merely instrumental in preparing us to be what we ought to be.

A Latter-day Saint professes to be a disciple of Jesus Christ. Indeed, the first principle of our religion is "faith in the Lord Jesus Christ." The second principle is repentance of things not consistent with faith in Christ. We bear witness to this faith by repentance and by humbling ourselves through baptism, as a witness that we are entering into a covenant to be followers of Christ "at all times and in all things, and in all places . . . even until death." (Mosiah 18:9.) Repentance and baptism "bringeth meekness, and lowliness of heart; and because of meekness and lowliness of heart cometh the visitation of the Holy Ghost, which Comforter filleth with hope and perfect love." (Moroni 8:26.) We renew the baptismal covenant each Sunday by partaking of the sacrament of the Lord's Supper in which we remember the Savior, take his name upon us, and witness that we will keep his commandments, that we might have his Spirit always to be with us. First, foremost, and always, a Latter-day Saint should be a disciple of Jesus Christ. The doctrines, rituals, practices, meetings, and fellowship of the Church have no other purpose than to build Christian lives of its members and to encourage the same among others. Divine authority, baptism, temple ordinances, and theological doctrines are not ends in themselves. They must be participated in and used in ways that promote Christian living among men.

The prophet Mormon speaks of infant baptism as "mockery before God" and "putting trust in dead works," because an infant can neither exercise faith in Christ nor repent to make the baptism efficacious (Moroni 2); the baptism of an adult is no less vain if that adult is not sincere in his striving to accept and follow Christ.

And what does it mean to follow Christ? The answer is

clear: "By this shall all men know that ye are my disciples, if ye have love one to another." (John 13:35.) Everything in the gospel depends on love. The most important thing a Latter-day Saint can do is love his neighbor—all of God's children, the poor, the sinner, the rich, the black, the Caucasian, the old, the young, the enemy, the widow, the orphan.

A disciple of Christ is not caught up in material things. He does not lay up for himself "treasures on earth," living in luxury while half the world goes to bed hungry. He uses his means and wealth to give employment, education, opportunity, even food to those in need.

A disciple of Christ is humble, meek, and lowly. He does not have all the answers; he asks, seeks, and knocks. He is not self-righteous. He is characterized by discontent over his own ignorance and sins and over the suffering of his fellowmen. He would gladly wash the feet of the wayfaring of mankind.

A disciple of Christ has faith in the Father. His faith is not born of self-interest, but, like that of Jesus, it is born of love and of trust in the Father's goodness and impartiality. His love of God, like all true love, is centered in the other person, in God.

I believe that the priesthood, the gift of the Holy Ghost, church organizations, and the teachings of the restored Church were given to men and women that they might become—and help others to become—true disciples of Christ. And, I repeat, if holding the priesthood does not teach and motivate a man to serve and love others more than he could and would without it, then amen to his priesthood. It is vain in his life, a bane rather than a blessing. "We have learned by sad experience that it is the nature and disposition of almost all men, as soon as they get a little authority, as they suppose, they will immediately begin to exercise unrighteous dominion. Hence many are called, but few are chosen. No power or influence can or ought to be maintained by virtue of the priesthood, only by persuasion, by long-suffering, by gentleness and meekness, and by love unfeigned; by kindness, and pure knowledge, which shall greatly enlarge the soul without hypocrisy, and without guile." (D&C 121:39-42.) "Let thy bowels also be full of charity towards all men, and to the household of faith, and let virtue garnish thy thoughts unceasingly; then shall thy confidence wax strong in the presence of God; and the doctrine of the priesthood shall distil upon thy soul as the dews of heaven." (D&C 121:45.)

Let The Church of Jesus Christ of Latter-day Saints be Christ's church not only because he established and endowed it as such on April 6, 1830, but because we Latter-day Saints follow Christ with humility and trust toward God and with feelings and deeds of love toward men.